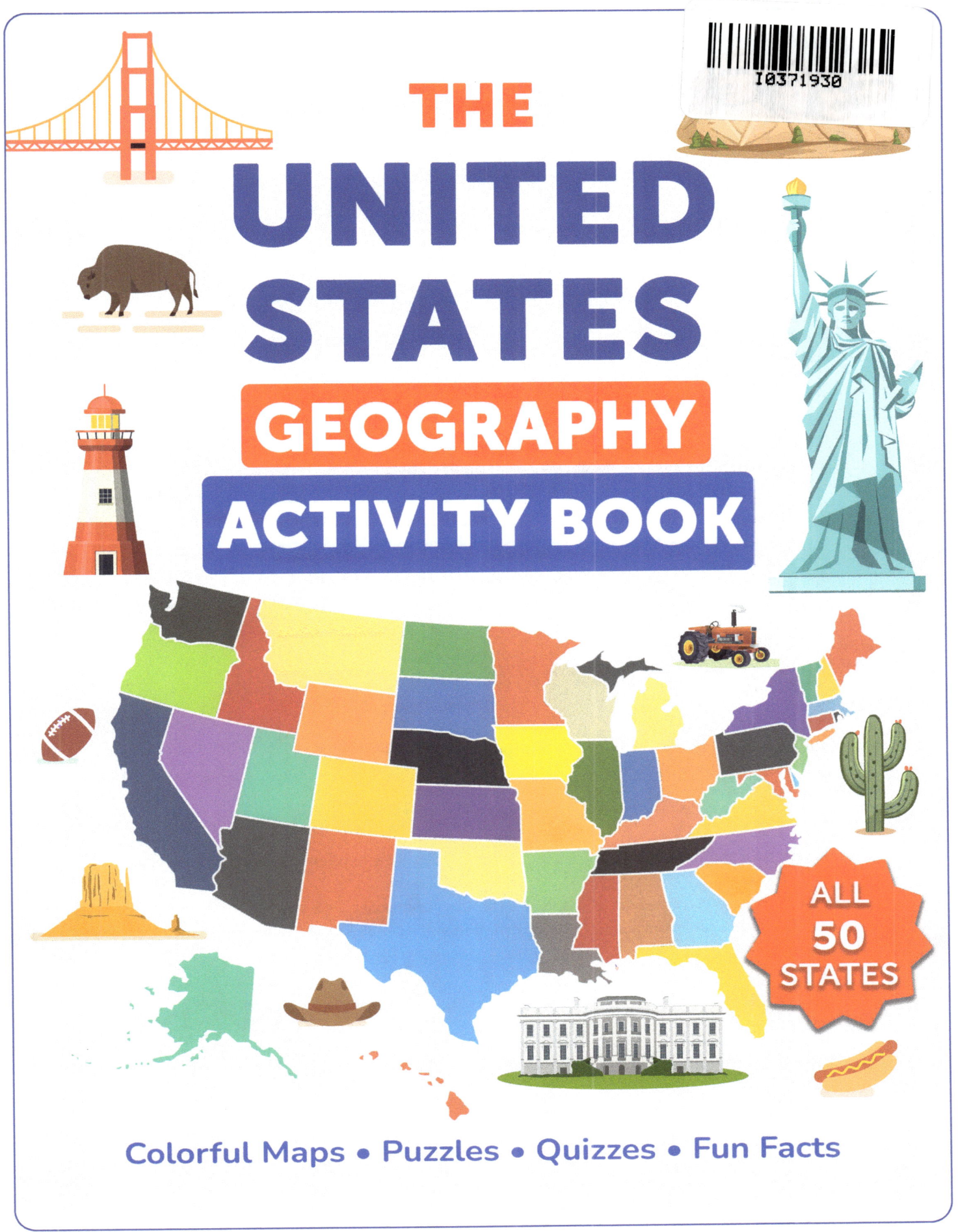

© 2026 Dylanna Publishing, Inc.
All rights reserved.

No part of this publication may be reproduced, stored in a retrieval system, or transmitted in any form or by any means—electronic, mechanical, photocopying, recording, or otherwise—without the prior written permission of the publisher, except in the case of brief quotations embodied in critical reviews and certain other noncommercial uses permitted by copyright law.

Trademarks: Dylanna Press is a registered trademark of Dylanna Publishing, Inc. and may not be used without written permission.

ISBN: 978-1-64790-447-0
Publisher: Dylanna Publishing, Inc.
First Edition: 2026
10 9 8 7 6 5 4 3 2 1

For information about special discounts for bulk purchases, please contact:

Dylanna Publishing, Inc.
www.dylannapublishing.com

Illustrations and photography: Licensed images & original artwork used under agreement.

This book is intended for educational and entertainment purposes. Every effort has been made to ensure the accuracy of information at the time of publication.

Welcome to the United States

From snowy mountains and sunny beaches to busy cities and quiet forests, the United States is full of amazing places to explore! In this book, you'll meet every state—its capital, symbols, and landmarks—plus discover fun facts and important moments in history. You'll also see how the country works and test your knowledge with mini quizzes. Whether you're learning at home or at school, this colorful book makes geography fun.

In this book, you'll:
- Explore iconic cities, national parks, and famous landmarks across all 50 states
- Learn about presidents, founding fathers, and key moments in early U.S. history
- Discover how America is divided into regions—and what makes each one unique
- Build map skills with state locators, symbols, borders, and fun geography challenges
- Play games, solve puzzles, try mazes, and test what you know with quick quizzes

Skills you'll build:
☐ Find states and regions on a U.S. map
☐ Name state capitals and abbreviations
☐ Recognize state symbols (bird, flower, animal)
☐ Describe landforms and landmarks
☐ Sequence key U.S. history events
☐ Explain the three branches of government

Capital vs. Capitol

Capital = the **city** where government meets.
Capitol = the **building** where lawmakers meet.

Quick Facts about the USA

- **Official name:** United States of America
- **Capital:** Washington, D.C.
- **Form of government:** Federal republic
- **Population:** About 342 million
- **Official language (federal):** English
- **National motto:** "In God We Trust."
- **National anthem:** "The Star-Spangled Banner"
- **Currency:** U.S. dollar

The United States at a Glance

The USA is made up of 50 states and spans from the Atlantic to the Pacific Ocean. The country also includes Alaska in the far northwest and Hawaii in the Pacific Ocean. States are grouped into four major regions: Northeast, South, Midwest, and West.

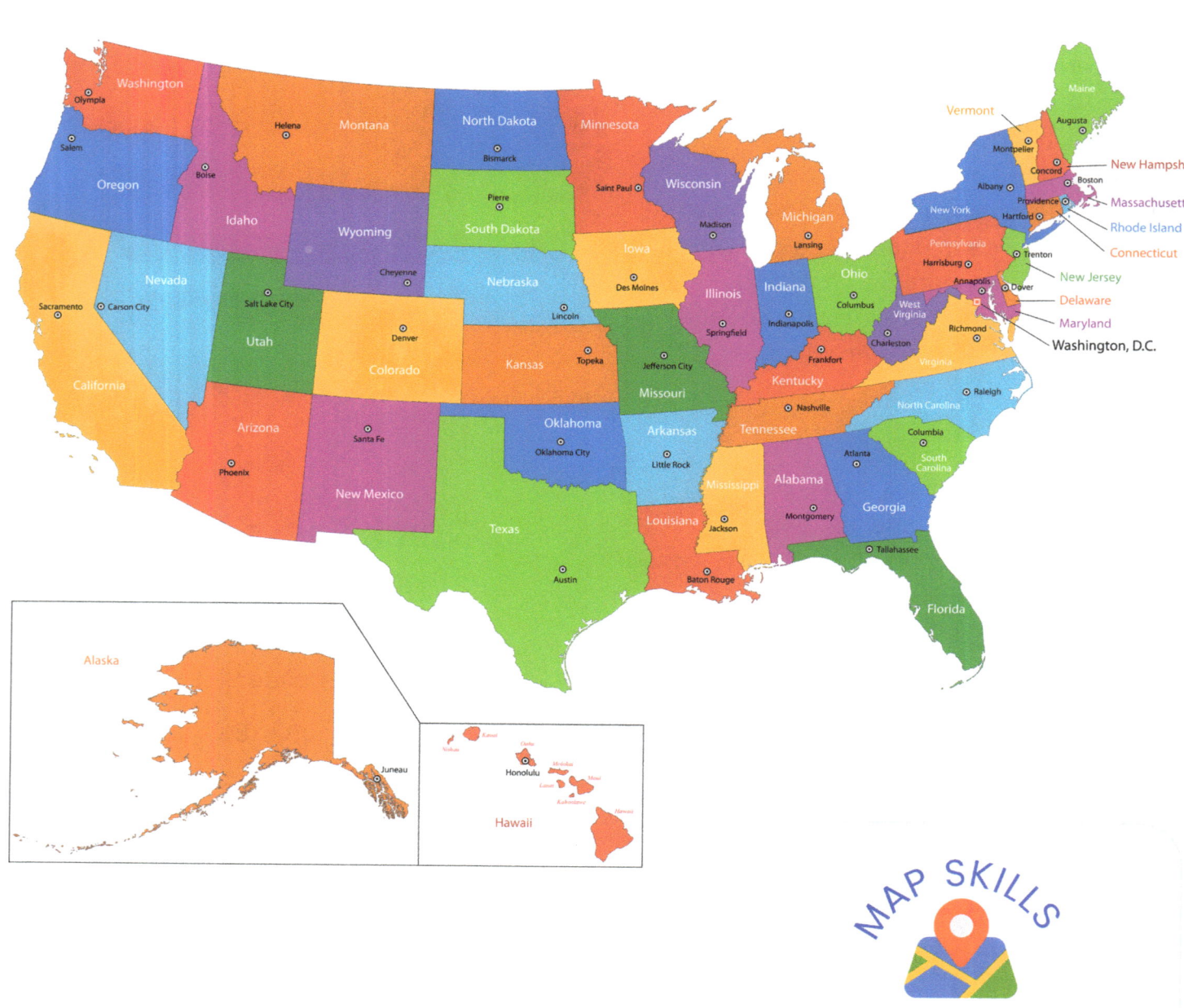

MAP SKILLS

Can you find your state on the map? Which states are next to it?

Symbols of a Nation

The flag of the United States is a powerful symbol of the nation's identity. Its 50 white stars stand for the 50 states, while the 13 red and white stripes recall the original colonies that declared independence in 1776. The flag is often called the "Stars and Stripes," and it has changed many times as new states joined the Union. Today's design was adopted in 1960 after Hawaii became the 50th state. Today, the flag serves as a reminder of America's history, unity, and ongoing story.

Great Seal of the United States

Source: U.S. Government, Public domain, via Wikimedia Commons

⭐ Pledge of Allegiance ⭐

The Pledge of Allegiance was first written in 1892. It has been slightly changed over the years, and the words "under God" were added in 1954. Today, many schools and events begin with this short promise of loyalty to the country.

I pledge allegiance to the Flag of the United States of America, and to the Republic for which it stands, one Nation under God, indivisible, with liberty and justice for all.

Branches of Government

The United States is a democracy, which means the people have the power to choose their leaders and help make decisions. To keep that power balanced, the government is divided into three branches: Executive, Legislative, and Judicial. Each branch has its own job, and together they make sure the country runs fairly and follows the Constitution.

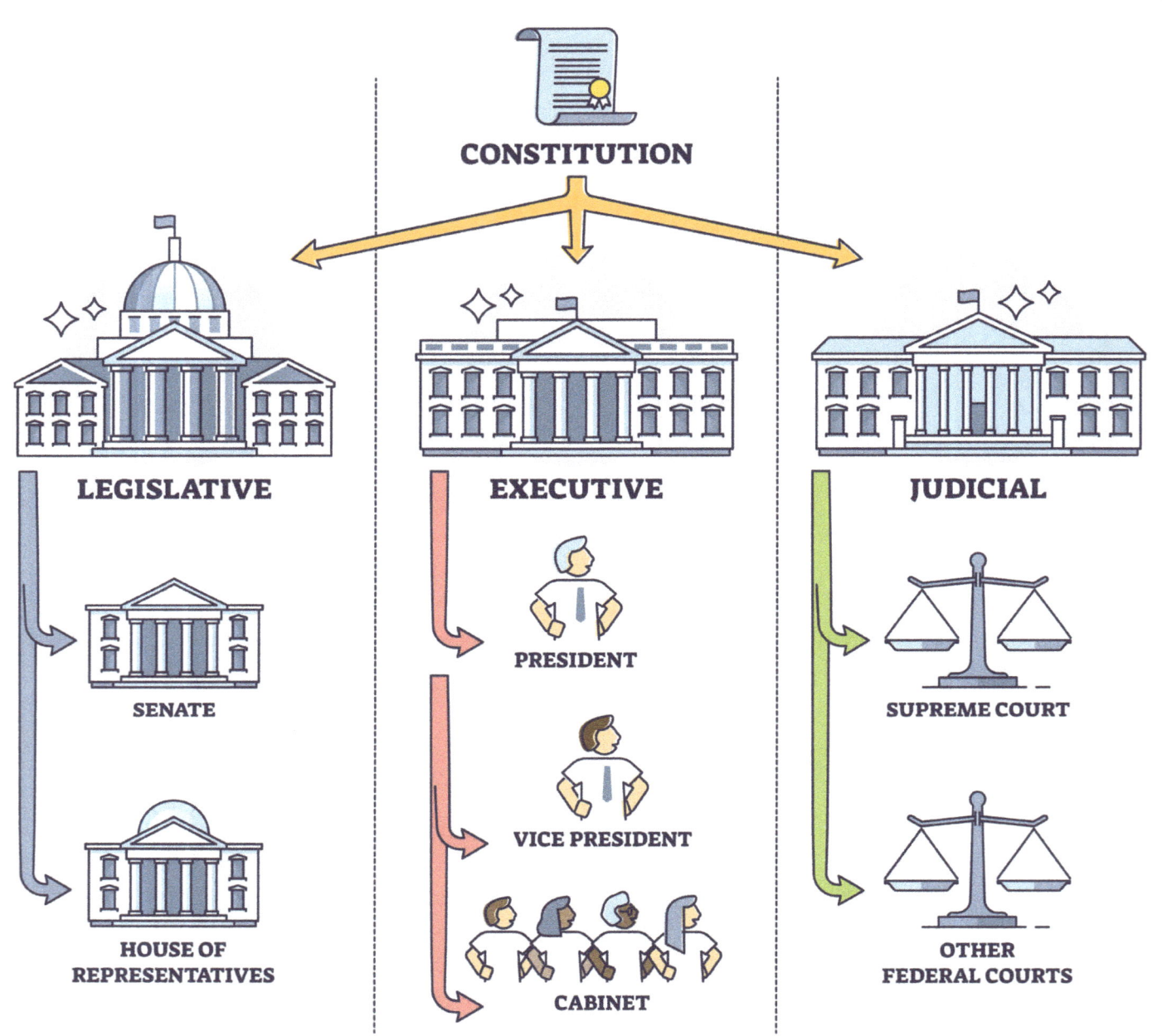

The **Legislative Branch** makes the laws. Congress is made up of two parts: the Senate and the House of Representatives. Senators and Representatives meet in the Capitol Building.

The **Executive Branch** carries out the laws and is led by the President. The President also serves as commander-in-chief of the armed forces and meets with leaders from other countries.

The **Judicial Branch** makes sure laws follow the Constitution. The Supreme Court is the highest court in the country and has nine justices.

Washington, D.C. — The Nation's Capital

Washington, D.C. was created to serve as the nation's capital, separate from any one state. It's where the President lives, where Congress makes laws, and where the Supreme Court meets. Millions of visitors come each year to see monuments like the Lincoln Memorial and the Washington Monument.

Washington, D.C. is not just about government — more than 700,000 people live there. The city has neighborhoods, schools, sports teams, and festivals just like any other place. People from many backgrounds call D.C. home, which makes it a diverse and vibrant city.

 ### Mini-Quiz – U.S. Government

1. How many branches of government are there?
   a) 2   b) 3   c) 4

2. Which branch makes the laws?
   a) Executive   b) Legislative   c) Judicial

3. Who lives in the White House?
   a) The President   b) Congress   c) The Supreme Court

4. What does the Judicial Branch do?
   a) Carries out the laws
   b) Decides if laws follow the Constitution
   c) Commands the military

5. **True or False:** Washington, D.C. is one of the 50 states.

U.S. Capitol Building

Did You Know? People who live in Washington, D.C. can vote for President, but they do not have voting senators or representatives in Congress.

Maze Fun!
Find the way from the White House to the Washington Monument.

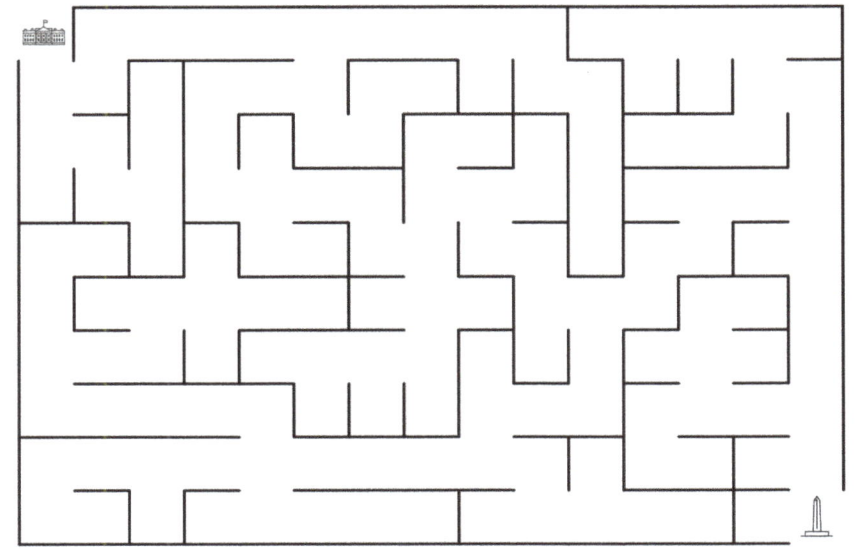

Quick Facts

- **Founded:** 1790
- **Named after** George Washington
- **Not a state** — it's a federal district
- **Located** on the Potomac River between Maryland and Virginia
- **Home to** the White House, Capitol, Supreme Court, and many national monuments

The Original 13 Colonies

Before the United States became a country, the land along the Atlantic Coast was divided into colonies controlled by Great Britain. Over time, thirteen colonies were established, stretching from Massachusetts in the north to Georgia in the south. People in these colonies spoke English, built towns, and worked the land, but they also wanted more freedom to make their own choices. These colonies eventually joined together to declare independence and form the United States of America.

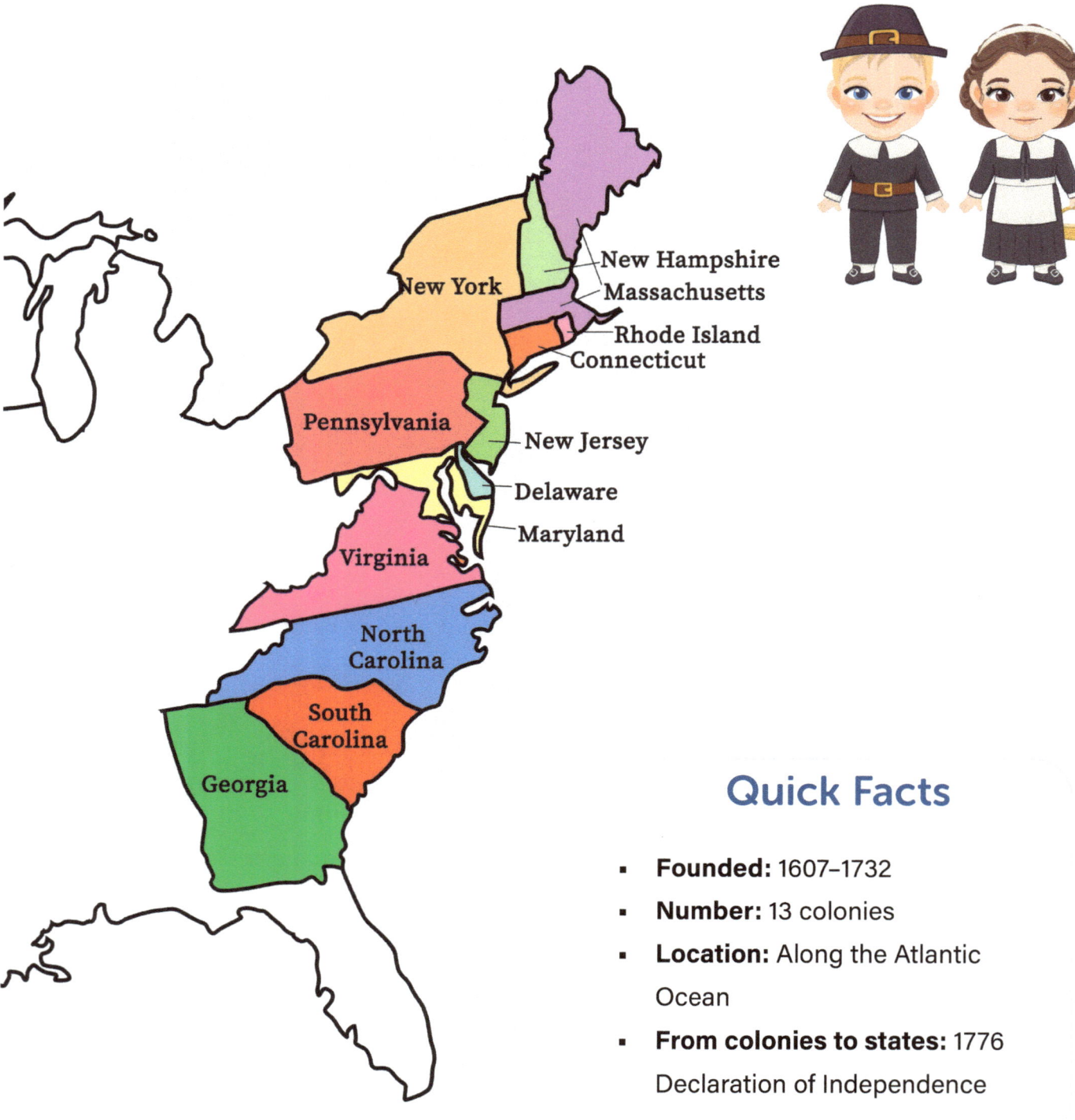

Quick Facts

- **Founded:** 1607–1732
- **Number:** 13 colonies
- **Location:** Along the Atlantic Ocean
- **From colonies to states:** 1776 Declaration of Independence

Independence and Founding Fathers

Declaration of Independence

On July 4, 1776, leaders from the colonies approved the Declaration of Independence, written mainly by Thomas Jefferson. It declared freedom from Britain and explained that all people have rights to life, liberty, and the pursuit of happiness. Americans celebrate this day every year as Independence Day.

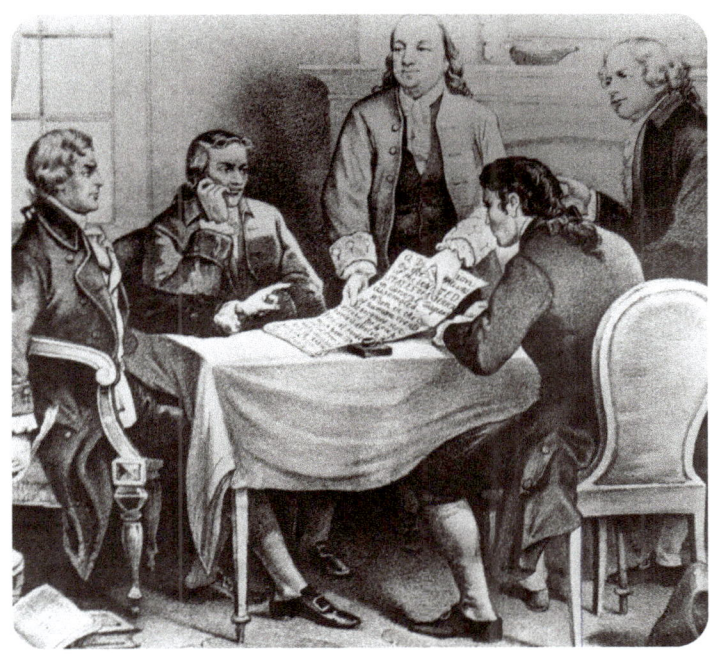

George Washington

George Washington led the Continental Army to victory in the American Revolution. People respected his honesty so much that he was chosen as the nation's first President. He loved farming at his home in Virginia, and today he's often called the "Father of His Country."

Thomas Jefferson

Thomas Jefferson wrote most of the Declaration of Independence, giving the colonies a voice for freedom. He later became the third President of the United States. Jefferson was also curious about science, built inventions, and collected books that helped start the Library of Congress.

? Who Am I ?

Read the clues and see if you can guess the person:

I didn't really have wooden teeth, but many of my false teeth were made from animal bone. Who am I?

I loved books so much that my collection helped start the Library of Congress. Who am I?

I flew a kite in a storm to study lightning and invented bifocals for reading. Who am I?

Benjamin Franklin

Benjamin Franklin was a writer, inventor, and diplomat. He flew a kite in a thunderstorm to study electricity, created the lightning rod, and started America's first public library. Franklin also helped convince France to support the colonies during the Revolution, which was a big reason the Americans won.

Borders and Neighbors

The United States is part of North America. It shares borders with Canada to the north and Mexico to the south. Oceans surround much of the country—the Atlantic to the east and the Pacific to the west. The Gulf of Mexico and the Great Lakes are also important waters.

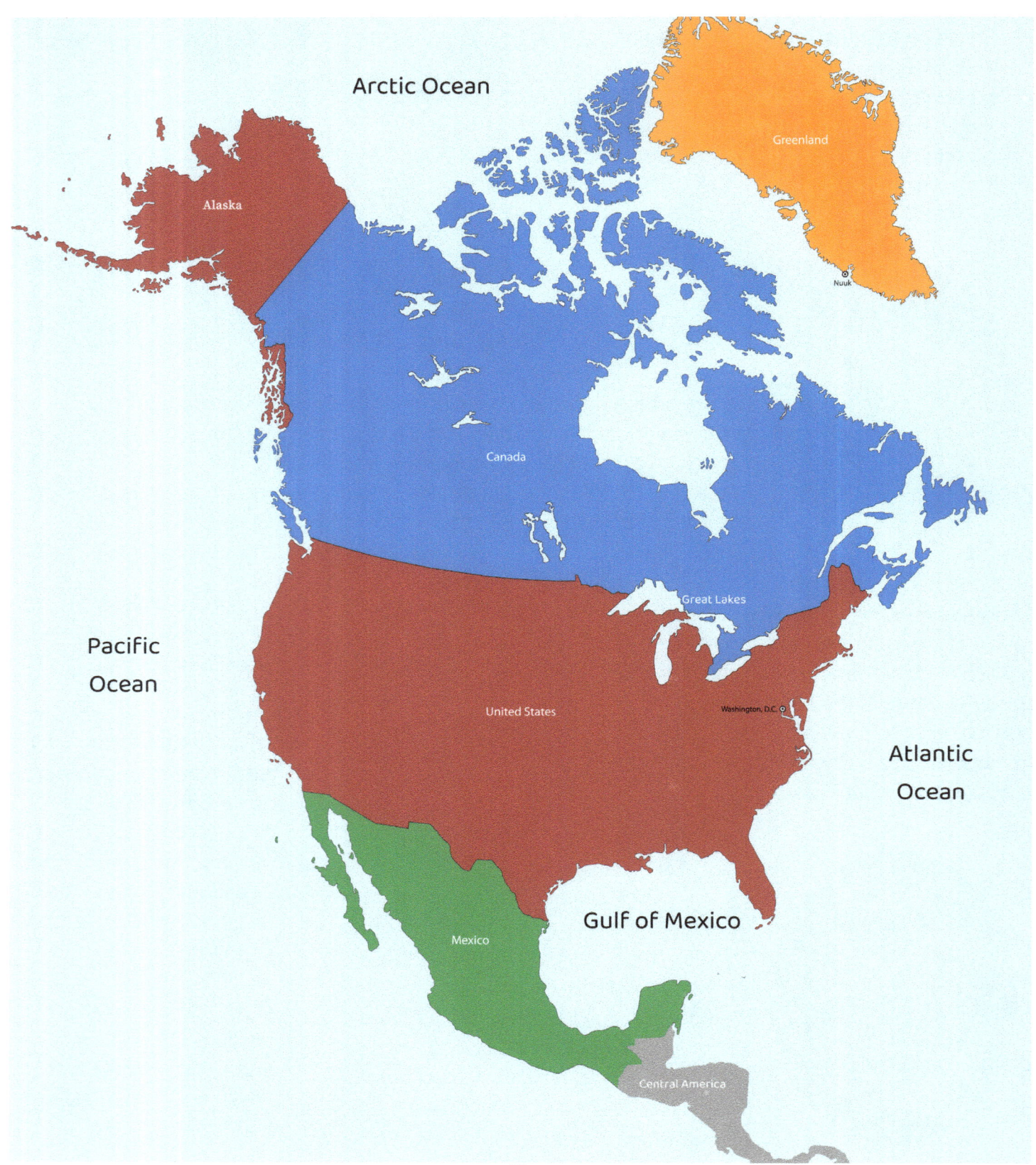

Map Quiz

Answer the questions using the map on the opposite page:

Which country is north of the United States?
a) Mexico   b) Canada   c) Brazil

Which ocean is on the east coast of the United States?
a) Pacific Ocean   b) Atlantic Ocean   c) Indian Ocean

Which ocean is on the west coast?
a) Atlantic Ocean   b) Pacific Ocean   c) Arctic Ocean

What body of water borders the southern coast near Florida?
a) Gulf of Mexico   b) Lake Superior   c) Hudson Bay

The United States shares its longest border with which country?
a) Mexico   b) Canada   c) Greenland

Did You Know? Alaska is farther west and farther east than any other state!

Maze Fun!
Find the way from North to South across the USA.

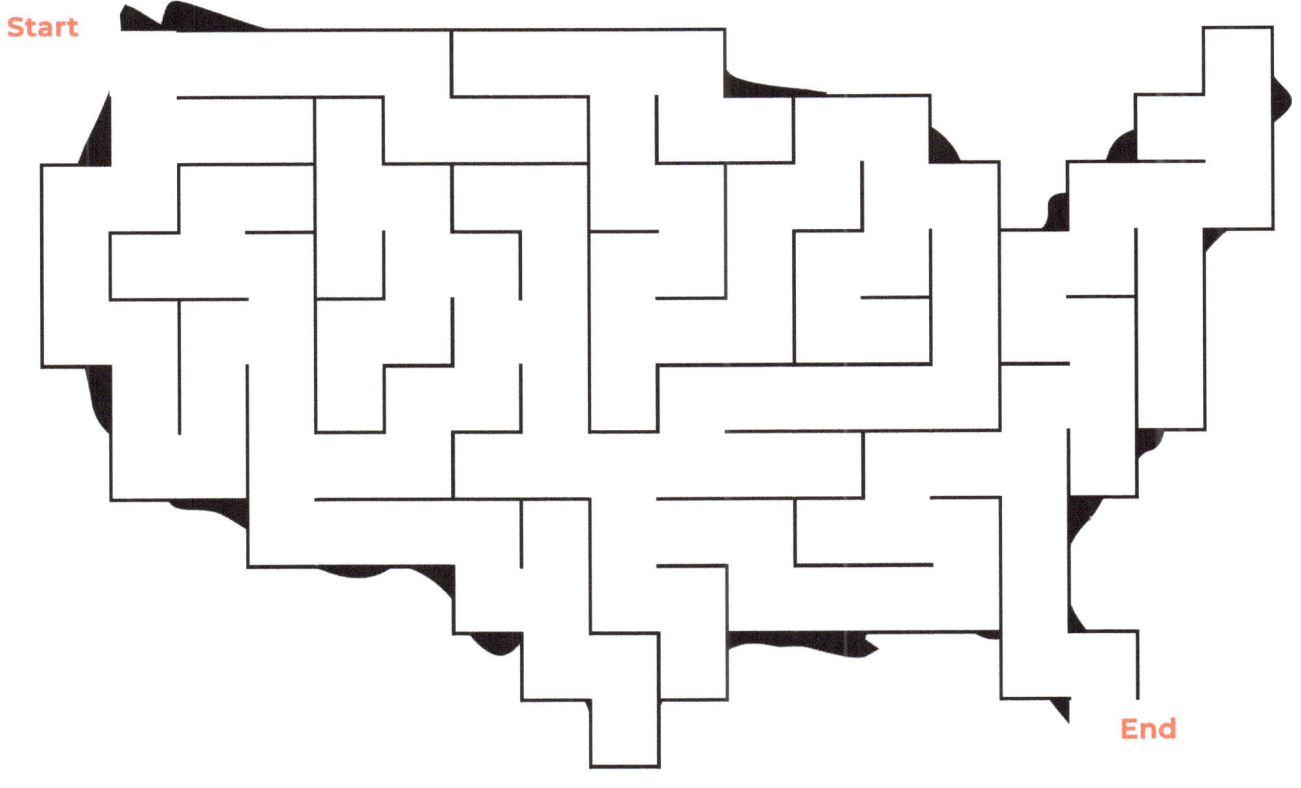

Symbols of America

A country's symbols tell a story about its history and values. The United States has animals, plants, and mottos that stand for freedom, strength, and unity. Here are a few of the most important ones!

Bald Eagle

Chosen in 1782, the bald eagle represents freedom and courage. Its sharp eyes and strong wings make it the perfect bird to symbolize the nation.

American Bison

In 2016, the American bison became the national mammal. Once nearly extinct, these powerful animals now live in many national parks, like Yellowstone.

Rose

The rose was named the national flower in 1986. Roses come in many colors and symbolize beauty, love, and honor.

Oak Tree

The oak tree became the national tree in 2004. Known for its strength and long life, it has shaded people in America for hundreds of years.

Motto: *E Pluribus Unum*
"Out of Many, One"

Crossword

Across

3 Ocean on the east coast (8)
6 Highest court in the land (7,5)
7 The Great _____, a group of five big lakes (5)
10 Building where Congress meets (7)
13 Building where the president lives (10)
15 U.S. capital city (10)
16 National flower (4)
17 Wrote most of the Declaration of Independence (9)

Down

1 Country north of United States (6)
2 National mammal (5)
4 Number of branches of government (5)
5 Country south of the U.S. (6)
8 Number of original colonies (8)
9 Ship that brought Pilgrims to Massachusetts (9)
11 Ocean on the west coast (7)
12 He flew a kite in a storm (8)
14 National bird (5)

13

The Presidents of the United States

Since 1789, the United States has had 47 presidents. Each leader has played an important role in guiding the country through challenges and changes. From George Washington, the first president, to today, the list of presidents shows the history of America's government and the people who have led it.

No.	Name	Years	No.	Name	Years
1	George Washington	1789–97	25	William McKinley	1897–1901
2	John Adams	1797–1801	26	Theodore Roosevelt	1901–09
3	Thomas Jefferson	1801–09	27	William H. Taft	1909–13
4	James Madison	1809–17	28	Woodrow Wilson	1913–21
5	James Monroe	1817–25	29	Warren G. Harding	1921–23
6	John Q. Adams	1825–29	30	Calvin Coolidge	1923–29
7	Andrew Jackson	1829–37	31	Herbert Hoover	1929–33
8	Martin Van Buren	1837–41	32	Franklin D. Roosevelt	1933–45
9	William H. Harrison	1841	33	Harry S. Truman	1945–53
10	John Tyler	1841–45	34	Dwight D. Eisenhower	1953–61
11	James K. Polk	1845–49	35	John F. Kennedy	1961–63
12	Zachary Taylor	1849–50	36	Lyndon B. Johnson	1963–69
13	Millard Fillmore	1850–53	37	Richard Nixon	1969–74
14	Franklin Pierce	1853–57	38	Gerald Ford	1974–77
15	James Buchanan	1857–61	39	Jimmy Carter	1977–81
16	Abraham Lincoln	1861–65	40	Ronald Reagan	1981–89
17	Andrew Johnson	1865–69	41	George H. W. Bush	1989–93
18	Ulysses S. Grant	1869–77	42	Bill Clinton	1993–2001
19	Rutherford B. Hayes	1877–81	43	George W. Bush	2001–09
20	James A. Garfield	1881	44	Barack Obama	2009–17
21	Chester A. Arthur	1881–85	45	Donald J. Trump	2017–21
22	Grover Cleveland	1885–89	46	Joe Biden	2021–25
23	Benjamin Harrison	1889–93	47	Donald J. Trump	2025–present
24	Grover Cleveland	1893–97			

⭐ Presidential Fun Facts ⭐

Youngest President: Theodore Roosevelt became president at just 42 years old!

Youngest Elected: John F. Kennedy was only 43 when he won the election.

Shortest Presidency: William Henry Harrison served just 31 days before he died.

Two-Timers: Grover Cleveland and Donald Trump are the only presidents to serve non-consecutive terms.

Tallest President: Abraham Lincoln stood 6 feet 4 inches tall — taller than most people at the time.

Heaviest President: William Howard Taft was so big that the White House bathtub had to be replaced to fit him!

Match the President to the Fact

1. Thomas Jefferson
2. John Quincy Adams
3. Franklin D. Roosevelt
4. Ronald Reagan
5. Barack Obama

A. First African American President
B. President during Great Depression
C. Made Louisiana Purchase
D. Son of a President who became President
E. Hollywood actor who became President

Design Your Own Coin!

Imagine you could design a new U.S. coin. Which president would you put on it? Draw the coin in the circles below, and write why you chose that person.

_____
_____
_____
_____
_____

Quiz: Who Was It?

1. Who was the first president?

2. Who was president during the Civil War?

3. Who started the national parks system?

4. Who gave the "Ask not what your country . . ." speech?

5. Who is the current president?

Word Search

Look for the hidden words in the puzzle below. Can you find them all?

```
N W J K N P B I S O N A O S E N
L P R E S I D E N T D I S C O X
I O D O F M Y D L P U E Q I H E
N T A S W F Z M K I R V T T C X
C T F Y H R E D A G B A E N M U
O O S A I U O R N N N E E A K L
L M E M T K E O S E T D R L H O
N J K B E Y C R S O N H X T R T
L F A W H X W O W E N P E A Y I
D I L V O L R R P L V X K M U P
E W T I U Y W E I S X E Z H S A
M Z A U S G D F B U T Q L Q E C
O K E J E N B E K D R X J T G E
C F R W I N O T G N I H S A W R
R L G S E I N O L O C Y Y G F S
A A C O N S T I T U T I O N O L
C G V F W V Z U O C I F I C A P
Y V D O L L A R E L G A E T Y I
```

Anthem	Dollar	Motto
Atlantic	Eagle	Nation
Bison	Flag	Pacific
Capitol	Great Lakes	President
Colonies	Independence	Roosevelt
Congress	Jefferson	Rose
Constitution	Liberty	Washington
Democracy	Lincoln	White House

Regions of the United States

The United States is made up of 50 states, and sometimes it helps to group them into regions. Each region has its own geography, history, and culture. Together, the four regions show just how diverse and exciting the country can be!

Northeast: Small but full of history. This region includes the first American colonies, big cities like New York and Boston, and beautiful mountains and coastlines.
States: Maine, New Hampshire, Vermont, Massachusetts, Rhode Island, Connecticut, New York, New Jersey, Pennsylvania

South: Known for warm weather, beaches, mountains, music, and Southern cooking. This region is also home to Washington, D.C., the nation's capital.
States: Delaware, Maryland, Virginia, West Virginia, Kentucky, North Carolina, South Carolina, Georgia, Florida, Alabama, Mississippi, Tennessee, Arkansas, Louisiana, Oklahoma, Texas

Midwest: America's "Heartland," with farms, rivers, and the Great Lakes.
States: Ohio, Indiana, Illinois, Michigan, Wisconsin, Minnesota, Iowa, Missouri, North Dakota, South Dakota, Nebraska, Kansas

West: A region of extremes: deserts, giant mountains, and landmarks like the Grand Canyon and Golden Gate Bridge.
States: Montana, Wyoming, Colorado, New Mexico, Arizona, Utah, Idaho, Washington, Oregon, California, Nevada, Alaska, Hawaii

Northeast Region

The Northeast is the smallest region in land area, but it's packed with history, people, and famous places. This is where the first American colonies were built and where you'll find big cities like New York, Boston, and Philadelphia.

Quick Facts

- Largest city: New York City
- Smallest state: Rhode Island
- Number of states: Nine
- Has four distinct seasons
- Long coastlines famous for fishing, shipping, and seafood

Maine, New Hampshire, Vermont, Massachusetts, Rhode Island, Connecticut, New York, Pennsylvania, New Jersey

History
The Northeast is where the United States began. Many of the original 13 colonies were here, and important events like the Boston Tea Party and the signing of the Declaration of Independence took place in this region.

Geography
From the rocky Atlantic coastline to the Appalachian Mountains, the Northeast has many landscapes packed into a small area. Winters are snowy, summers are warm, and the region is famous for colorful fall leaves.

Culture
The Northeast is full of busy cities like New York, Boston, and Philadelphia, but it also has small towns and farms. The region is known for fresh seafood, maple syrup, famous universities, and lots of music, art, and sports.

Match the Landmark!
Match each Northeast landmark to its state:

Statue of Liberty   _____

Liberty Bell   _____

Boston Tea Party   _____

Maple Syrup   _____

Connecticut

Connecticut may be small, but it has a big history. Known as the "Constitution State," it helped shape America's government. Today, it's famous for its shoreline towns, beautiful forests, and world-class universities.

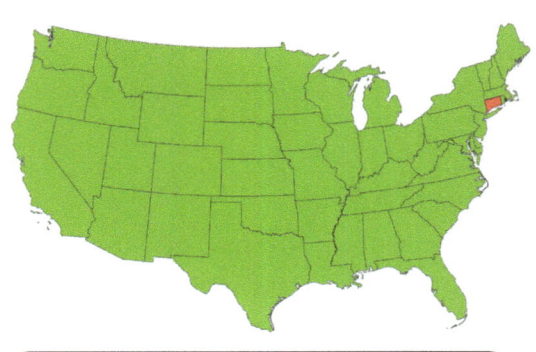

Quick Facts

- ⭐ **Capital:** Hartford
- 🧭 **Abbreviation:** CT
- 👥 **Population:** ~3.6 million
- 📅 **Statehood:** 1788 (5th)
- 🏷️ **Nickname:** The Constitution State
- 🐦 **Bird:** American Robin
- 🌸 **Flower:** Mountain Laurel
- 🐢 **Animal:** Sperm Whale
- 📍 **Famous Sites:** Mystic Seaport, Yale University, Mark Twain House

DID YOU KNOW?
The first hamburger in America was served in New Haven, Connecticut in 1895!

Mountain laurel

American robin

State flag

Maine

Maine is the northeasternmost state in the U.S. and famous for its rocky coastline, lighthouses, and delicious lobster. Much of the state is covered in forests, making it a great place for hiking, camping, and spotting moose.

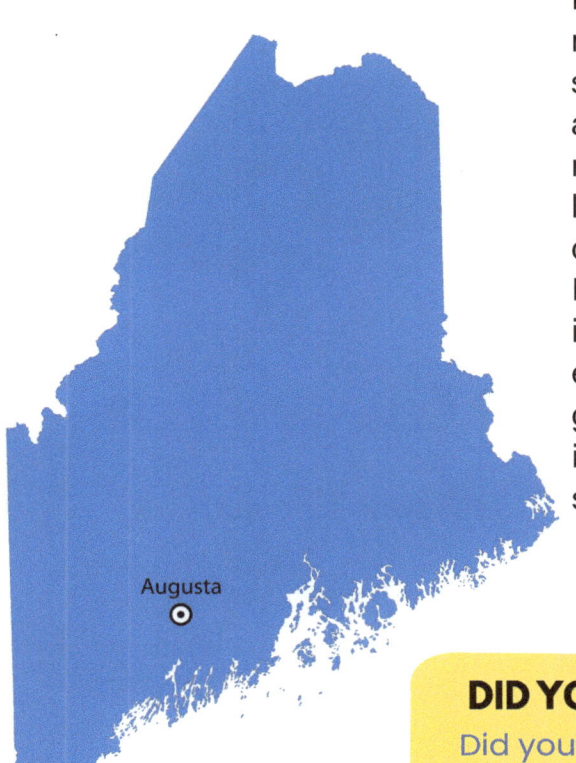

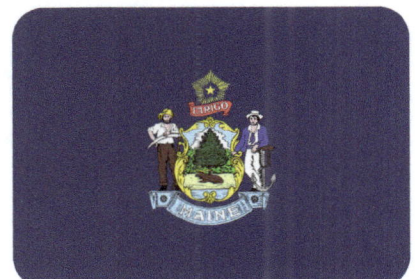

DID YOU KNOW?
Did you know? Maine has more coastline than California — over 3,400 miles when you count all its bays and inlets!

Quick Facts

- ⭐ **Capital:** Augusta
- 🧭 **Abbreviation:** ME
- 👥 **Population:** ~1.4 million
- 📅 **Statehood:** 1820 (23rd)
- 🏷️ **Nickname:** The Pine Tree State
- 🐦 **Bird:** Chickadee
- 🌸 **Flower:** White Pine Cone and Tassel
- 🐢 **Animal:** Moose
- 📍 **Famous Sites:** Acadia National Park, Portland Head Light

Chicakadee

Moose

State flag

Massachusetts

Massachusetts played a key role in America's founding. From the Pilgrims at Plymouth Rock to the Boston Tea Party, history is everywhere. Today, it's known for top universities, sports teams, and colorful fall scenery.

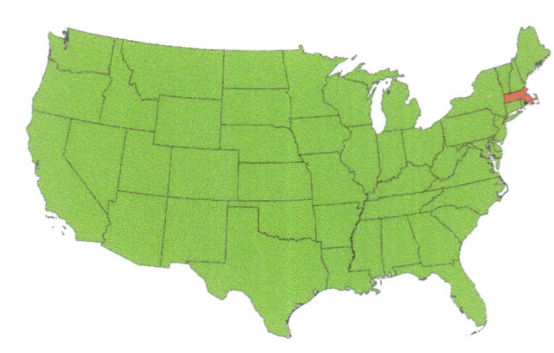

DID YOU KNOW?

Boston built the very first subway system in the United States back in 1897.

Quick Facts

- ⭐ **Capital:** Boston
- 🧭 **Abbreviation:** MA
- 👥 **Population:** ~7 million
- 📅 **Statehood:** 1788 (6th)
- 🏷️ **Nickname:** The Bay State
- 🐦 **Bird:** Black-Capped Chickadee
- 🌸 **Flower:** Mayflower
- 🐢 **Animal:** Right Whale
- 📍 **Famous Sites:** Boston Tea Party Ships, Plymouth Rock, Harvard University

Black-capped chickadee

Right Whale

State flag

22

New Hampshire

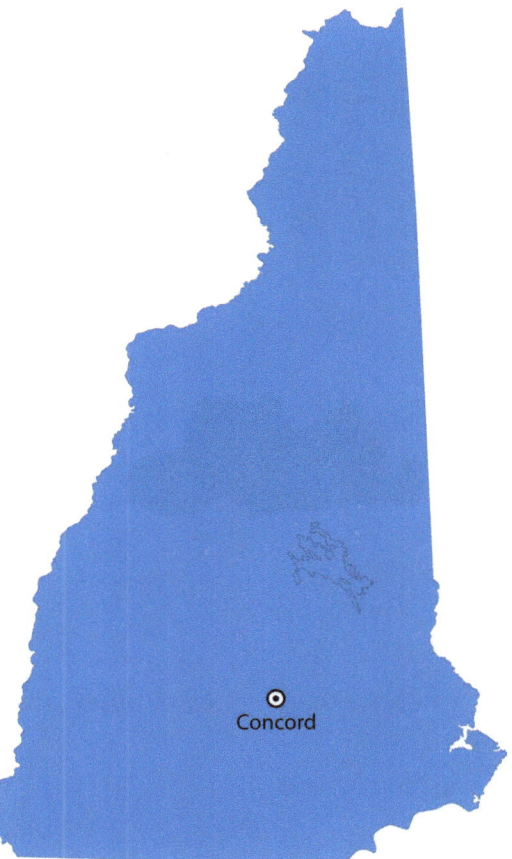

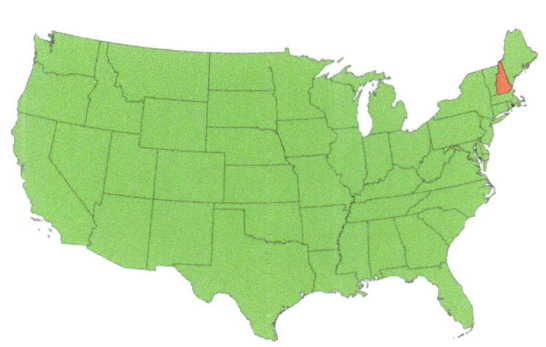

New Hampshire is known for its mountains, forests, and small-town charm. The White Mountains are popular for skiing and hiking, and the state motto — "Live Free or Die" — shows its independent spirit.

Quick Facts

- ⭐ **Capital:** Concord
- 🧭 **Abbreviation:** NH
- 👥 **Population:** ~1.4 million
- 📅 **Statehood:** 1788 (9th)
- 🏷️ **Nickname:** The Granite State
- 🐦 **Bird:** Purple Finch
- 🌸 **Flower:** Purple Lilac
- 🐢 **Animal:** White-Tailed Deer
- 📍 **Famous Sites:** White Mountains, Lake Winnipesaukee

DID YOU KNOW? The first free public library in America opened in Peterborough, New Hampshire, in 1833.

White-Tailed Deer

Purple Finch

State flag

New Jersey

New Jersey is one of the most densely populated states, but it's also full of beaches, farms, and forests. The Jersey Shore is famous for boardwalks and ocean fun, while cities like Newark and Trenton have rich history.

DID YOU KNOW?
The very first baseball game was played in Hoboken, New Jersey, in 1846!

Quick Facts

- ⭐ **Capital:** Trenton
- 🧭 **Abbreviation:** NJ
- 👤 **Population:** ~9.3 million
- 📅 **Statehood:** 1787 (3rd)
- 🏷️ **Nickname:** The Garden State
- 🐦 **Bird:** Eastern Goldfinch
- 🌸 **Flower:** Violet
- 🐢 **Animal:** Horse
- 📍 **Famous Sites:** Atlantic City Boardwalk, Liberty State Park

Eastern Goldfinch

Violet

State flag

New York

New York is one of the most exciting states in America. It's home to the nation's biggest city — New York City — and natural wonders like Niagara Falls and the Adirondack Mountains. The state truly has something for everyone.

DID YOU KNOW?
The New York State Fair in Syracuse is the oldest state fair in America — it started in 1841!

Quick Facts

⭐ **Capital:** Albany

🧭 **Abbreviation:** NY

👥 **Population:** ~19.5 million

📅 **Statehood:** 1788 (11th)

🏷️ **Nickname:** The Empire State

🐦 **Bird:** Eastern Bluebird

🌸 **Flower:** Rose

🐢 **Animal:** Beaver

📍 **Famous Sites:** Statue of Liberty, Niagara Falls, Adirondack Mountains

Eastern Bluebird

Beaver

State flag

25

Pennsylvania

Pennsylvania is packed with American history. It's where the Declaration of Independence was signed and where the Liberty Bell still stands. The state is also famous for farmland, mountains, and chocolate from the town of Hershey.

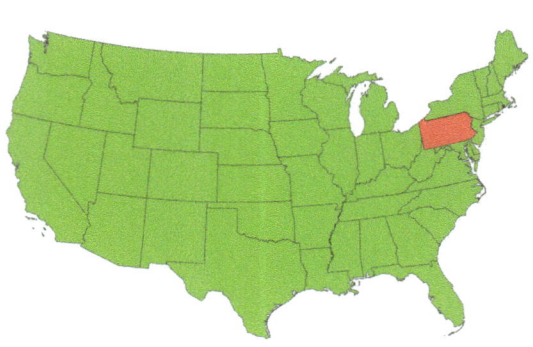

Harrisburg

DID YOU KNOW?
Pennsylvania is home to the nation's very first zoo — the Philadelphia Zoo opened in 1874.

Quick Facts

- ⭐ **Capital:** Harrisburg
- 🧭 **Abbreviation:** PA
- 👤 **Population:** ~13 million
- 📅 **Statehood:** 1787 (2nd)
- 🏷️ **Nickname:** The Keystone State
- 🐦 **Bird:** Ruffed Grouse
- 🌸 **Flower:** Mountain Laurel
- 🐢 **Animal:** White-Tailed Deer
- 📍 **Famous Sites:** Liberty Bell, Gettysburg, Hershey

Ruffed Grouse

White-Tailed Deer

State flag

Rhode Island

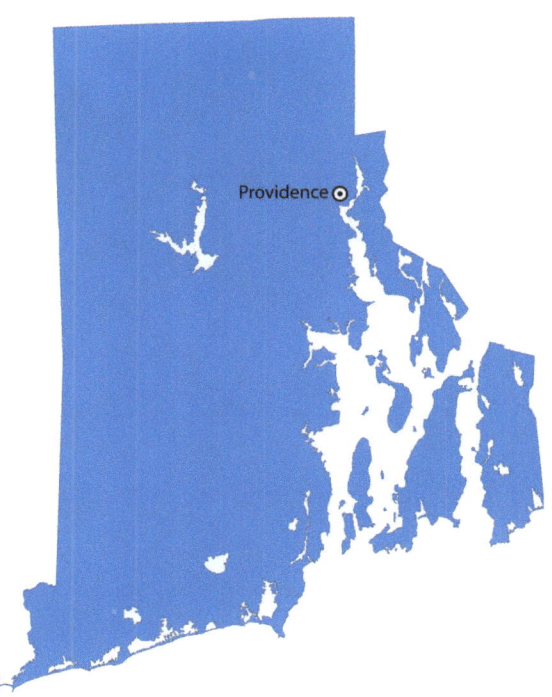

Rhode Island may be the smallest state, but it has over 400 miles of coastline! Known as the "Ocean State," it's famous for sailing, beaches, and seafood. Its capital, Providence, is filled with art and history.

DID YOU KNOW? Rhode Island was the last of the original 13 colonies to join the United States, in 1790.

Quick Facts

- ⭐ **Capital:** Providence
- 🧭 **Abbreviation:** RI
- 👥 **Population:** ~1.1 million
- 📅 **Statehood:** 1790 (13th)
- 🏷️ **Nickname:** The Ocean State
- 🐦 **Bird:** Rhode Island Red
- 🌸 **Flower:** Violet
- 🐢 **Animal:** Harbor Seal
- 📍 **Famous Sites:** Newport Mansions, Narragansett Bay

Violet

Harbor Seal

State flag

Vermont

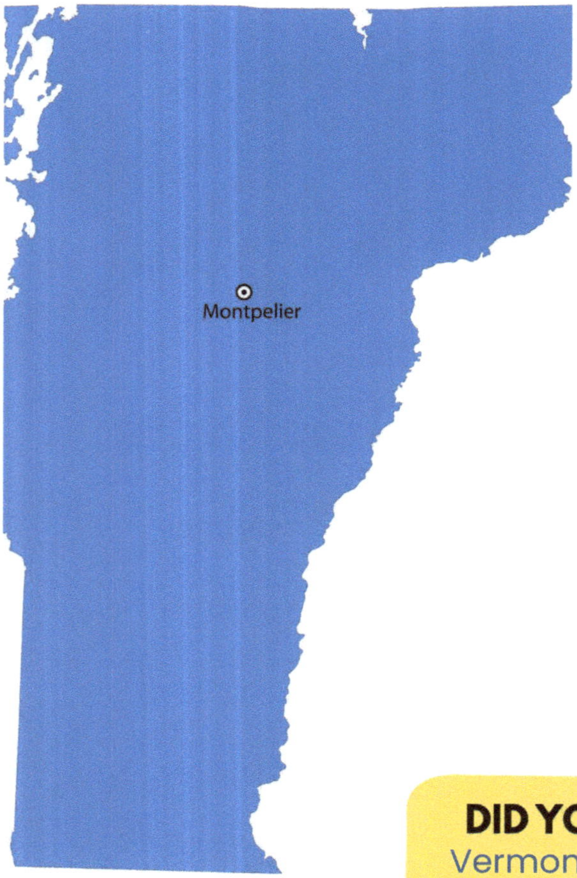

Vermont is known for its mountains, maple syrup, and covered bridges. It was the first state to join the Union after the original 13 colonies. With its forests and small towns, Vermont is a perfect place to see colorful fall leaves.

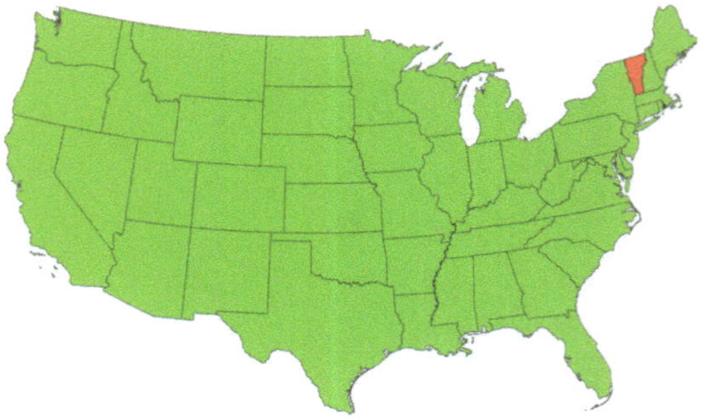

DID YOU KNOW? Vermont has no billboards along its highways. The state banned them to protect its beautiful scenery!

Quick Facts

- ⭐ **Capital:** Montpelier
- 🧭 **Abbreviation:** VT
- 👤 **Population:** ~650,000
- 📅 **Statehood:** 1791 (14th)
- 🏷️ **Nickname:** The Green Mountain State
- 🐦 **Bird:** Hermit Thrush
- 🌸 **Flower:** Red Clover
- 🐢 **Animal:** Morgan Horse
- 📍 **Famous Sites:** Green Mountains, Ben & Jerry's Factory, Stowe

Morgan horse

Hermit thrush

State flag

Maze Craze

Help the lighthouse keeper get to the top of the lighthouse.

Finish

Word Search

Look for the hidden words in the puzzle below. Can you find them all?

```
U I X K E S U O H T H G I L D
A P A I N A V L Y S N N E P E
T H T E P N V E R M O N T R N
L I Y R D R O C N O C O E F R
A L N I E N O T S O B I C O Q
N A A H S N B V U J L R B S C
T D B S Q C T C I E C R T I E
I E L P C Y F O P D A T Z T I
C L A M P O B T N H E V I U Y
C P A A R I N C E S H N G N E
L H T H S O N N U M A R C T S
N I S W M A T H E R A X Z E R
E A U E J F C K G C Y P E H E
W U G N N A J C O A T Q L E J
Y O U L S E E N I A M I I E W
O T A S T A F O R E S T C O E
R H A R R I S B U R G C L U N
K M R R H O D E I S L A N D T
```

Albany	Harbor	New Jersey
Atlantic	Harrisburg	New York
Augusta	Lighthouse	Pennsylvania
Boston	Maine	Philadelphia
Concord	Maple	Providence
Connecticut	Massachusetts	Rhode Island
Forest	Montpelier	Trenton
Granite	New Hampshire	Vermont

Matching Game

Match the state with its bird or animal

- Maine
- Rhode Island
- Vermont
- New Hampshire
- New York
- Pennsylvania
- Massachusetts
- Connecticut
- New Jersey

Beaver · American Robin · Harbor Seal · Morgan Horse · Purple Finch · Right Whale · Ruffed Grouse · Eastern Goldfinch · Moose

South Region

The South is one of the largest and most diverse regions of the United States. From sunny beaches to rolling mountains, it's full of history, music, and traditions that have shaped the nation. Warm weather, rich farmland, and unique cultures make the South stand out.

Delaware, Maryland, Virginia, West Virginia, Kentucky, North Carolina, South Carolina, Georgia, Florida, Alabama, Mississippi, Tennessee, Arkansas, Louisiana, Oklahoma, Texas

Quick Facts

- Largest City: Houston, Texas
- Climate: Hot summers, mild winters; hurricanes in coastal areas
- Nickname: Often called the "Sun Belt"
- Fun Fact: The South is the birthplace of jazz, blues, country, and rock 'n' roll!

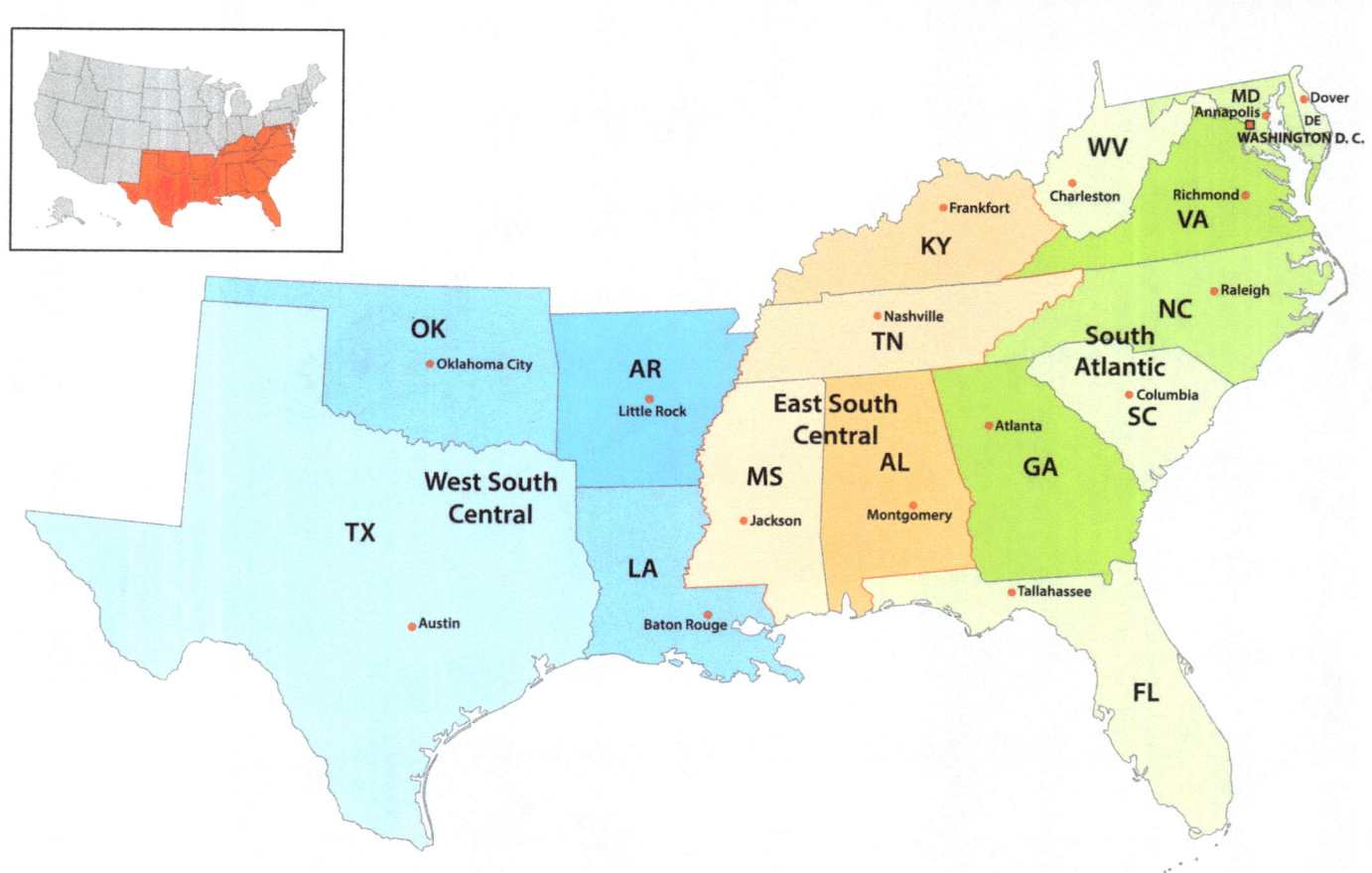

History
The South has a long and complex history. It was home to many of the first English settlements, and later played a central role in the Civil War. Historic cities like Charleston, New Orleans, and Atlanta still show the region's past.

Charleston, SC

Geography
The South is known for warm weather, long coastlines, and fertile farmland. The Appalachian Mountains run through the northern part, while beaches and the Gulf of Mexico define the southern edge. Hurricanes sometimes affect this region.

Culture
From country music to jazz and blues, the South has influenced American music like no other region. It's also famous for Southern cooking — think fried chicken, barbecue, and cornbread — and for traditions like rodeos and Mardi Gras.

Match the Landmark!
Match each Southern landmark to its state:

The Alamo   _____

Everglades   _____

Martin Luther
King Jr. Memorial   _____

Mardi Gras   _____

33

Alabama

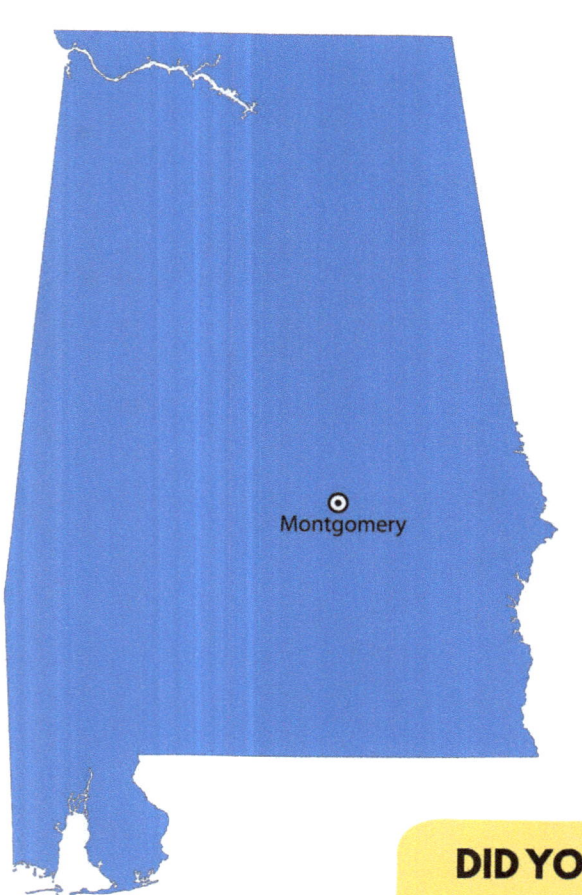

Alabama is known for its rich history, from the Civil Rights Movement to its musical roots. With rolling hills, rivers, and a warm climate, it's great for farming and outdoor fun. The state is also famous for Southern hospitality and college football!

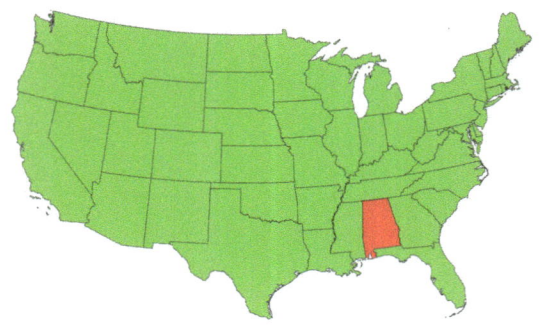

Quick Facts

⭐ **Capital:** Montgomery

🧭 **Abbreviation:** AL

👤 **Population:** ~5.1 million

📅 **Statehood:** 1819 (22nd)

🏷️ **Nickname:** The Heart of Dixie

🐦 **Bird:** Northern Flicker

🌸 **Flower:** Camellia

🐢 **Animal:** Black Bear

📍 **Famous Sites:** U.S. Space & Rocket Center, Birmingham Civil Rights District

DID YOU KNOW?
The first rocket to send humans to the moon was built in Huntsville, Alabama!

Northern flicker

Black bear

State flag

Arkansas

Arkansas is called "The Natural State" because of its mountains, forests, and hot springs. The Ozark Mountains are perfect for hiking, and Hot Springs National Park is full of natural wonders. It's a beautiful mix of nature and small-town charm.

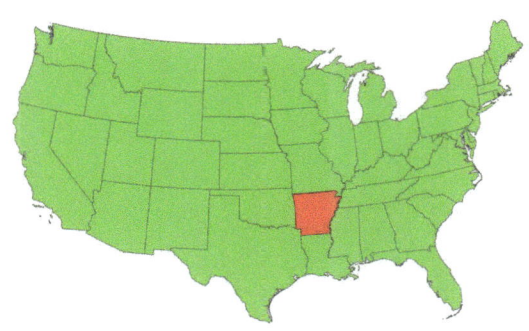

Quick Facts

- ⭐ **Capital:** Little Rock
- 🧭 **Abbreviation:** AR
- 👤 **Population:** ~3 million
- 📅 **Statehood:** 1836 (25th)
- 🏷️ **Nickname:** The Natural State
- 🐦 **Bird:** Northern Mockingbird
- 🌸 **Flower:** Apple Blossom
- 🐢 **Animal:** White-Tailed Deer
- 📍 **Famous Sites:** Hot Springs National Park, Ozark Mountains

White-tailed deer

DID YOU KNOW?

Arkansas is the only state where you can dig for real diamonds — at Crater of Diamonds State Park.

Northern mockingbird

State flag

Delaware

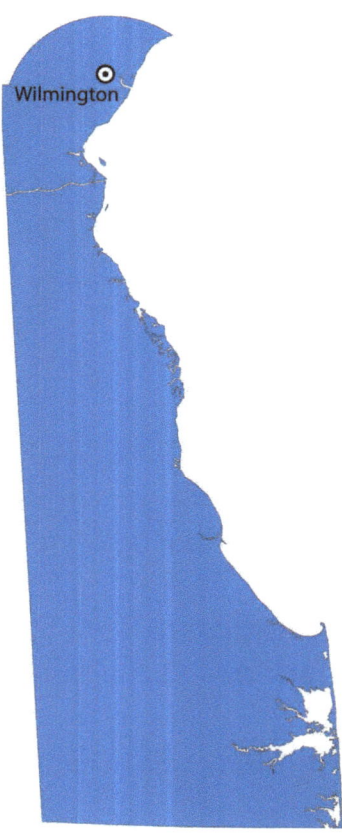

Delaware is the second smallest state but full of history — it was the first to sign the U.S. Constitution! The state has sandy beaches, small towns, and tax-free shopping. It's sometimes called "The First State" for a reason.

DID YOU KNOW?
Delaware has no sales tax, so shoppers from other states love to visit for tax-free deals!

Quick Facts

⭐ **Capital:** Dover

🧭 **Abbreviation:** DE

👤 **Population:** ~1 million

📅 **Statehood:** 1787 (1st)

🏷️ **Nickname:** The First State

🐦 **Bird:** Blue Hen Chicken

🌸 **Flower:** Peach Blossom

🐢 **Animal:** Grey Fox

📍 **Famous Sites:** Rehoboth Beach, Dover International Speedway

Peach blossom

Blue hen chicken

State flag

Florida

Florida is famous for sunshine, beaches, and theme parks. It's home to the Everglades, NASA's Kennedy Space Center, and miles of coastline. From oranges to alligators, Florida is full of color and adventure year-round.

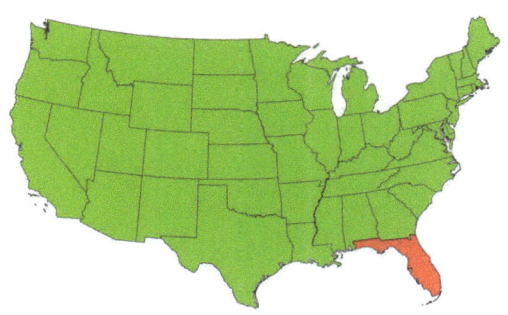

DID YOU KNOW?
Florida has more golf courses than any other state — over 1,000 of them!

Quick Facts

- ⭐ **Capital:** Tallahassee
- 🧭 **Abbreviation:** FL
- 👤 **Population:** ~22 million
- 📅 **Statehood:** 1845 (27th)
- 🏷️ **Nickname:** The Sunshine State
- 🐦 **Bird:** Mockingbird
- 🌸 **Flower:** Orange Blossom
- 🐢 **Animal:** Florida Panther
- 📍 **Famous Sites:** Everglades, Kennedy Space Center, Walt Disney World

Florida panther

Orange blossom

State flag

Georgia

Georgia is known for peaches, sweet tea, and Southern charm. The state's capital, Atlanta, played a key role in the Civil Rights Movement and is now a major modern city. Mountains, beaches, and farmland make Georgia beautifully diverse.

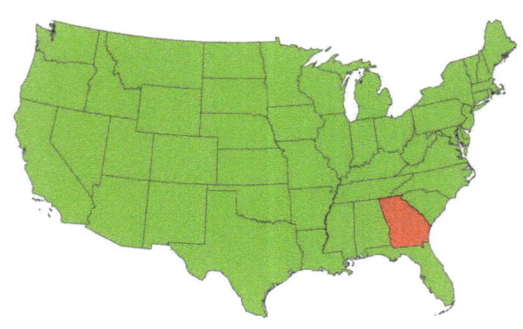

DID YOU KNOW?

Coca-Cola was invented in Atlanta, Georgia, in 1886.

Quick Facts

⭐ **Capital:** Atlanta

🧭 **Abbreviation:** GA

👥 **Population:** ~11 million

📅 **Statehood:** 1788 (4th)

🏷️ **Nickname:** The Peach State

🐦 **Bird:** Brown Thrasher

🌸 **Flower:** Cherokee Rose

🐢 **Animal:** White-Tailed Deer

📍 **Famous Sites:** Stone Mountain, Martin Luther King Jr. National Historic Site

White-tailed deer

Brown thrasher

State flag

Kentucky

Kentucky is the land of bluegrass music, horse racing, and rolling hills. The Kentucky Derby is the most famous horse race in the world! The state is also known for bourbon, caves, and warm Southern traditions.

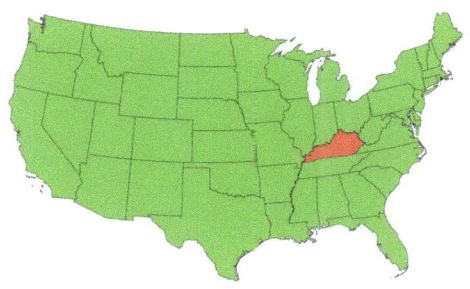

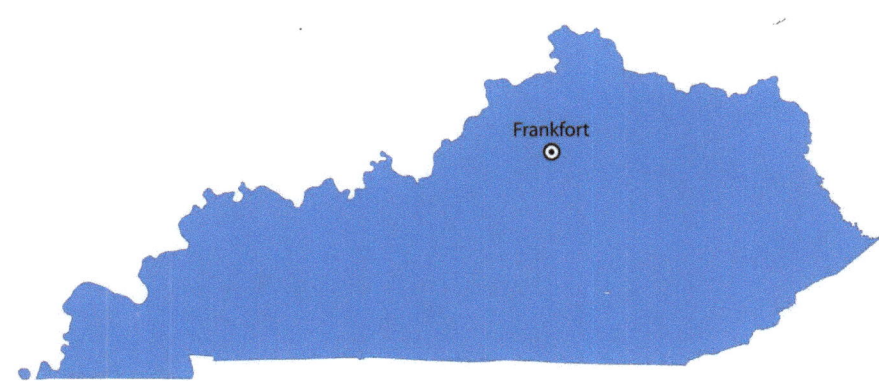

Quick Facts

- ⭐ **Capital:** Frankfort
- 🧭 **Abbreviation:** KY
- 👤 **Population:** ~4.5 million
- 📅 **Statehood:** 1792 (15th)
- 🏷️ **Nickname:** The Bluegrass State
- 🐦 **Bird:** Northern Cardinal
- 🌸 **Flower:** Goldenrod
- 🐢 **Animal:** Horse
- 📍 **Famous Sites:** Mammoth Cave, Churchill Downs, Bourbon Trail

DID YOU KNOW?
The Kentucky Derby is the longest-running horse race in the world — it's been held every year since 1875!

Goldenrod

Northern cardinal

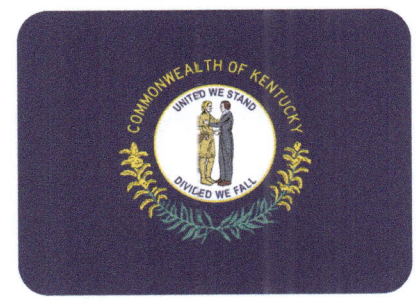

State flag

39

Louisiana

Louisiana is bursting with culture, music, and flavor. Its largest city, New Orleans, is famous for jazz, Mardi Gras, and spicy Cajun food. With the Mississippi River and the bayous, the state has a rhythm all its own.

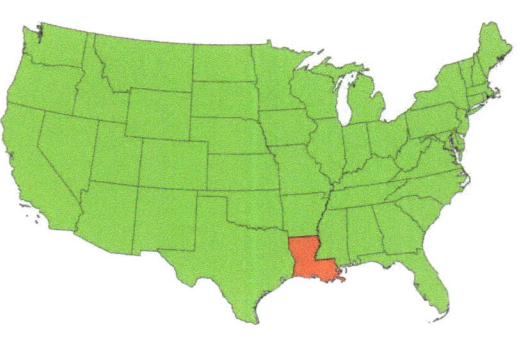

Quick Facts

- ⭐ **Capital:** Baton Rouge
- 🧭 **Abbreviation:** LA
- 👤 **Population:** ~4.6 million
- 📅 **Statehood:** 1812 (18th)
- 🏷️ **Nickname:** The Pelican State
- 🐦 **Bird:** Brown Pelican
- 🌸 **Flower:** Magnolia
- 🐢 **Animal:** Alligator
- 📍 **Famous Sites:** French Quarter, Mardi Gras, Bayous

Brown pelican

DID YOU KNOW?

Louisiana is home to more alligators than people — there are over 2 million in the state!

Alligator

State flag

Maryland

Maryland may be small, but it's packed with variety — from beaches on the Atlantic coast to mountains in the west. It's known for blue crabs, sailing on Chesapeake Bay, and historic sites in Baltimore and Annapolis.

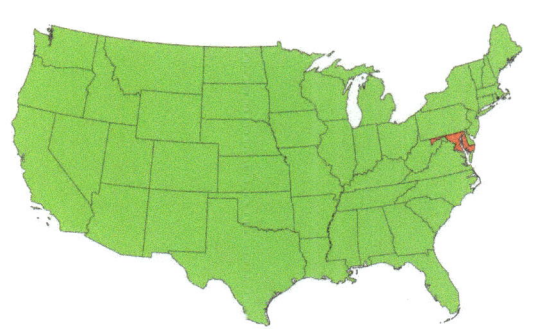

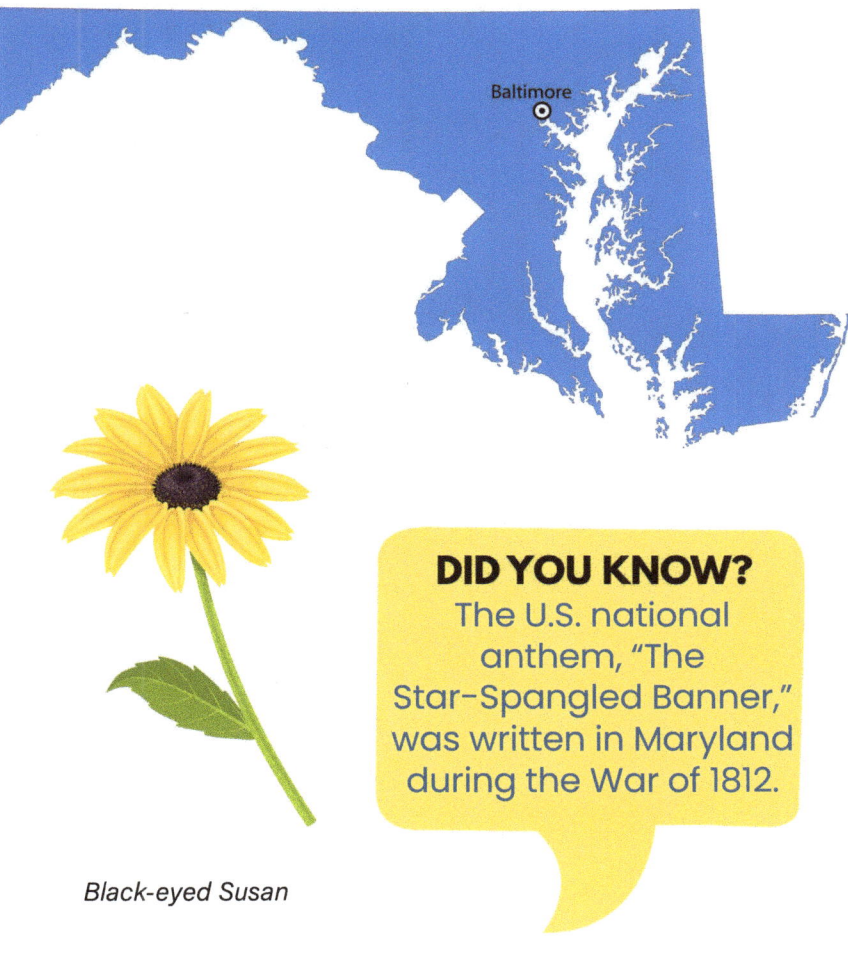

Black-eyed Susan

DID YOU KNOW? The U.S. national anthem, "The Star-Spangled Banner," was written in Maryland during the War of 1812.

Quick Facts

- ⭐ **Capital:** Annapolis
- 🧭 **Abbreviation:** MD
- 👥 **Population:** ~6.2 million
- 📅 **Statehood:** 1788 (7th)
- 🏷️ **Nickname:** The Old Line State
- 🐦 **Bird:** Baltimore Oriole
- 🌸 **Flower:** Black-Eyed Susan
- 🐢 **Animal:** Blue Crab
- 📍 **Famous Sites:** Chesapeake Bay, Fort McHenry, Baltimore Harbor

Baltimore oriole

State flag

Mississippi

Mississippi is full of Southern history and culture. It's the birthplace of blues music and known for its riverboats and hospitality. Cotton fields, magnolia trees, and the mighty Mississippi River shape life in this beautiful state.

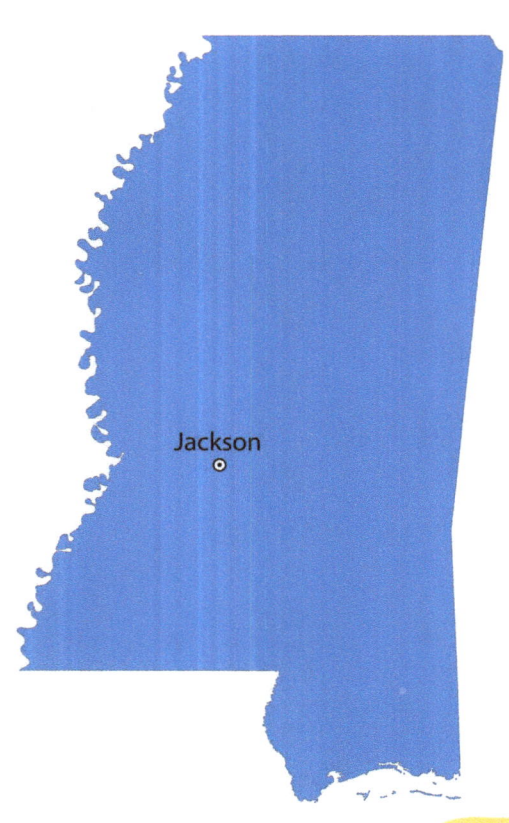

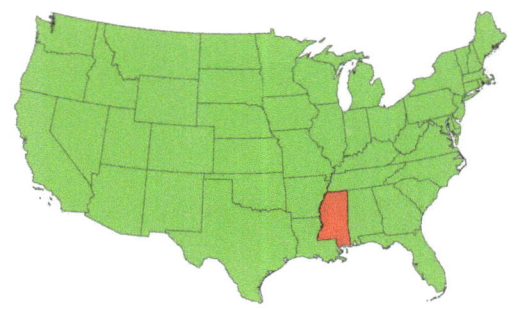

Quick Facts

- ⭐ **Capital:** Jackson
- 🧭 **Abbreviation:** MS
- 👤 **Population:** ~3 million
- 📅 **Statehood:** 1817 (20th)
- 🏷️ **Nickname:** The Magnolia State
- 🐦 **Bird:** Mockingbird
- 🌸 **Flower:** Magnolia
- 🐢 **Animal:** White-Tailed Deer and Red Fox
- 📍 **Famous Sites:** Vicksburg, Natchez Trace Parkway, Blues Trail

DID YOU KNOW?
The world's first heart transplant was performed in Mississippi in 1964.

Mockingbird

Red fox

State flag

North Carolina

North Carolina stretches from sandy beaches to tall mountain peaks. It's famous for the Wright brothers' first flight, NASCAR racing, and delicious barbecue. The state blends outdoor beauty with a growing modern economy.

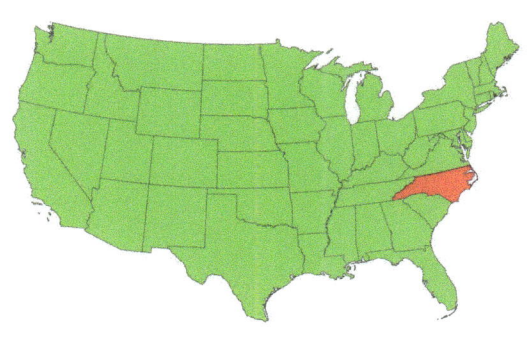

Quick Facts

- ⭐ **Capital:** Raleigh
- 🧭 **Abbreviation:** NC
- 👥 **Population:** ~10.8 million
- 📅 **Statehood:** 1789 (12th)
- 🏷️ **Nickname:** The tar Heel State
- 🐦 **Bird:** Northern Cardinal
- 🌸 **Flower:** Dogwood
- 🐢 **Animal:** Gray Squirrel
- 📍 **Famous Sites:** Great Smoky Mountains, Outer Banks, Kitty Hawk

DID YOU KNOW?
The Wright brothers made the first successful airplane flight in Kitty Hawk, North Carolina, in 1903.

Northern cardinal

Gray squirrel

State flag

43

Oklahoma

Oklahoma is known for wide-open plains, Native American heritage, and dramatic sunsets. It's called the "Sooner State" for settlers who arrived early during land runs. Tornadoes are common here, but so are strong communities and country pride.

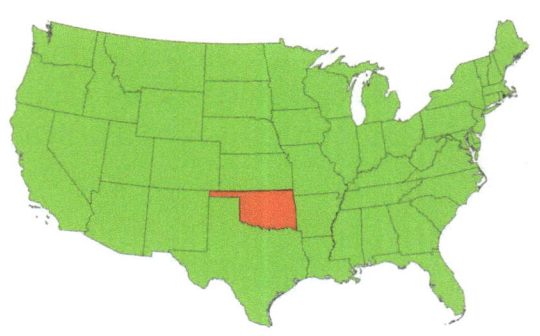

Scissor-tailed flycatcher

DID YOU KNOW?
Oklahoma has more man-made lakes than any other state — over 200!

Quick Facts

- ⭐ **Capital:** Oklahoma City
- 🧭 **Abbreviation:** OK
- 👤 **Population:** ~4 million
- 📅 **Statehood:** 1907 (46th)
- 🏷️ **Nickname:** The Sooner State
- 🐦 **Bird:** Scissor-Tailed Flycatcher
- 🌸 **Flower:** Oklahoma Rose
- 🐢 **Animal:** American Bison
- 📍 **Famous Sites:** Route 66, National Cowboy & Western Heritage Museum

State flag

American bison

South Carolina

South Carolina is one of the original 13 colonies and full of Southern charm. It's famous for historic Charleston, beautiful beaches, and warm weather. Palmetto trees and sweet tea are symbols of life in the Palmetto State.

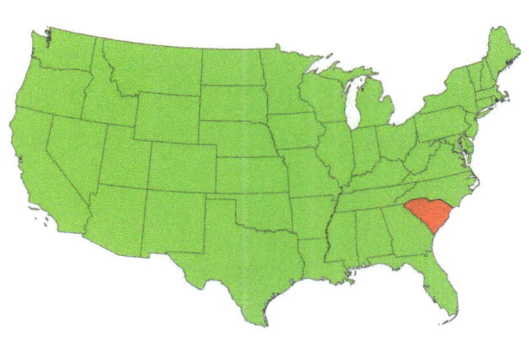

Quick Facts

- ⭐ **Capital:** Columbia
- 🧭 **Abbreviation:** SC
- 👥 **Population:** ~5.4 million
- 📅 **Statehood:** 1788 (8th)
- 🏷️ **Nickname:** The Palmetto State
- 🐦 **Bird:** Carolina Wren
- 🌸 **Flower:** Yellow Jessamine
- 🐢 **Animal:** White-Tailed Deer
- 📍 **Famous Sites:** Charleston, Fort Sumter, Myrtle Beach

Carolina wren

DID YOU KNOW?
The first shots of the Civil War were fired at Fort Sumter in Charleston Harbor, South Carolina.

White-tailed deer

State flag

Tennessee

Tennessee is all about music and mountains. Nashville is the heart of country music, while Memphis gave the world blues and rock 'n' roll. The Great Smoky Mountains add scenic beauty to this lively Southern state.

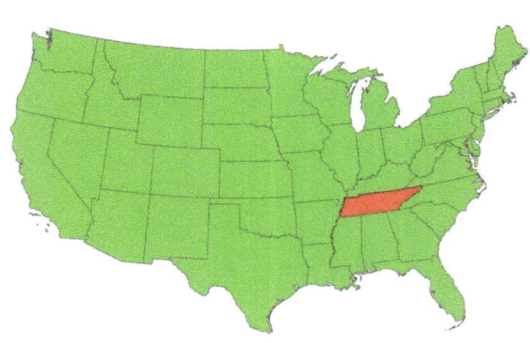

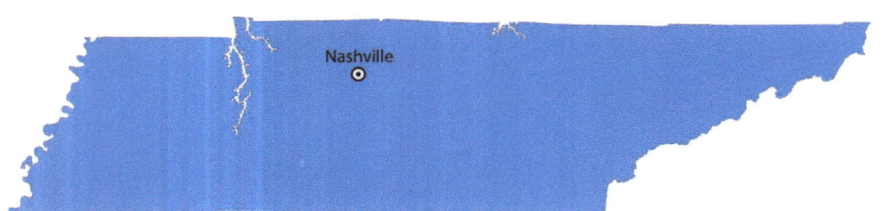

Quick Facts

- ⭐ **Capital:** Nashville
- 🧭 **Abbreviation:** TN
- 👤 **Population:** ~7.2 million
- 📅 **Statehood:** 1796 (16th)
- 🏷️ **Nickname:** The Volunteer State
- 🐦 **Bird:** Mockingbird
- 🌸 **Flower:** Iris
- 🐢 **Animal:** Raccoon
- 📍 **Famous Sites:** Graceland, Great Smoky Mountains, Grand Ole Opry

Iris

DID YOU KNOW?
Elvis Presley recorded his first song at Sun Studio in Memphis, Tennessee.

Raccoon

State flag

Texas

Everything's bigger in Texas! The state is huge — full of deserts, ranches, cities, and coastline. Texans are proud of their independence, their food (especially barbecue), and their cowboy spirit. The Alamo is one of its most famous landmarks.

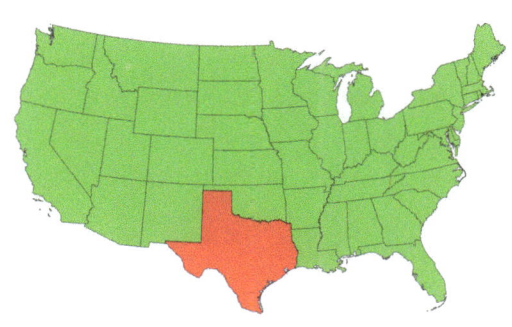

DID YOU KNOW?
Texas was an independent country for almost 10 years before joining the United States in 1845.

Mockingbird

Longhorn

Quick Facts

- ⭐ **Capital:** Austin
- 🧭 **Abbreviation:** TX
- 👤 **Population:** ~30 million
- 📅 **Statehood:** 1845 (28th)
- 🏷️ **Nickname:** The Lone Star State
- 🐦 **Bird:** Mockingbird
- 🌸 **Flower:** Bluebonnet
- 🐢 **Animal:** Longhorn
- 📍 **Famous Sites:** The Alamo, Big Bend National Park, NASA Houston

State flag

Virginia

Virginia is steeped in history — it's where the first English settlers arrived and where many U.S. presidents were born. With mountains, beaches, and colonial towns, it's both beautiful and educational. Its nickname, the "Old Dominion," reflects its proud heritage.

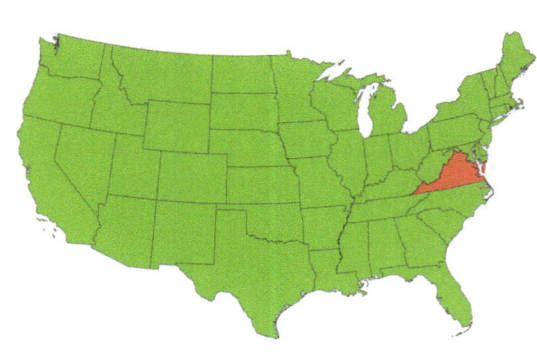

Quick Facts

- ⭐ **Capital:** Richmond
- 🧭 **Abbreviation:** VA
- 👥 **Population:** ~8.8 million
- 📅 **Statehood:** 1788 (10th)
- 🏷️ **Nickname:** The Old Dominion
- 🐦 **Bird:** Northern Cardinal
- 🌸 **Flower:** Dogwood
- 🐢 **Animal:** American Foxhound
- 📍 **Famous Sites:** Colonial Williamsburg, Mount Vernon, Shenandoah National Park

Dogwood

DID YOU KNOW?
More U.S. presidents were born in Virginia than in any other state — eight in total!

Northern cardinal

State flag

West Virginia

West Virginia is known for its rugged mountains, coal mining heritage, and outdoor adventure. The Appalachian Mountains offer hiking, rafting, and incredible fall scenery. Its small towns and friendly people give it a warm, welcoming spirit.

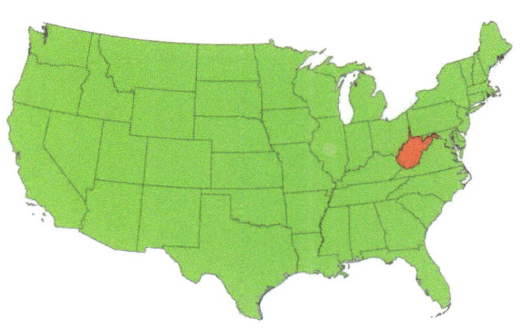

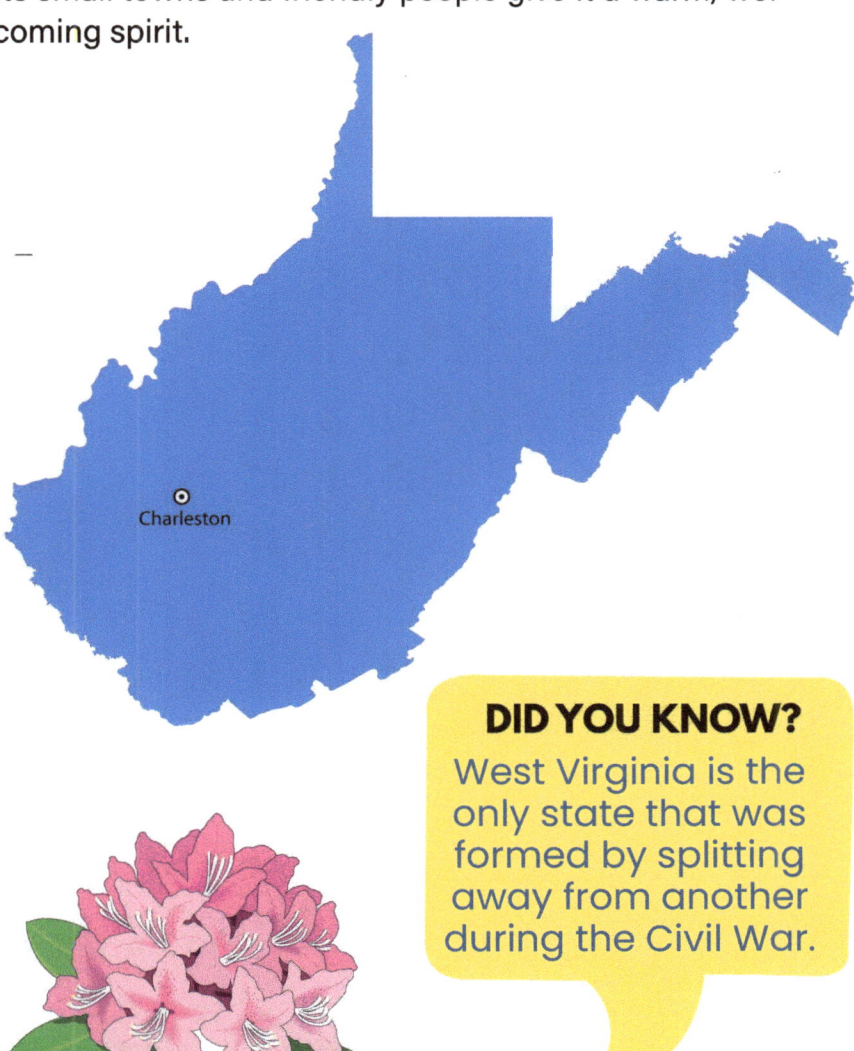

Quick Facts

- ⭐ **Capital:** Charleston
- 🧭 **Abbreviation:** WV
- 👤 **Population:** ~1.8 million
- 📅 **Statehood:** 1863 (35th)
- 🏷️ **Nickname:** The Mountain State
- 🐦 **Bird:** Northern Cardinal
- 🌸 **Flower:** Rhododendron
- 🐢 **Animal:** Black Bear
- 📍 **Famous Sites:** New River Gorge, Harpers Ferry, Seneca Rocks

DID YOU KNOW?
West Virginia is the only state that was formed by splitting away from another during the Civil War.

Rhododendron

Black bear

State flag

Word Search

Look for the hidden words in the puzzle below. Can you find them all?

```
P F A G B A T O N R O U G E F
R A L E I G H N Y S S A X E T
R A A O F M A O V O Q N E D X
M J B R F A T T Y U B I A A S
J I A G N R N S I T F I N N A
M N M I A Y A E R H W D I A S
A I A A S L L I C Q E L I N
D T S Y H A T R C A Y L O S A
I S X S V N A A H R K A R I K
R U H R I D J H M O C W A U R
O A W C L S Z C O L U A C O A
L O I G L Z S S N I T R H L D
F J U S E R K I D N N E T R J
A M O H A L K O P A E W R T B
J V I R G I N I A P K E O L M
E E S S E N N E T R I I N W E
F M O N T G O M E R Y L M F V
G S T A I N I G R I V T S E W
```

Alabama	Georgia	Oklahoma
Arkansas	Kentucky	Raleigh
Atlanta	Louisiana	Richmond
Austin	Maryland	South Carolina
Baton Rouge	Mississippi	Tennessee
Charleston	Montgomery	Texas
Delaware	Nashville	Virginia
Florida	North Carolina	West Virginia

Maze Craze

Help the cowboy find his way through the cowboy boot.

51

Which State Am I?

Read each clue and write the name of the state it describes.

1 I'm famous for my peaches and hosted the 1996 Summer Olympics.
   Which state am I? _____

2 Jazz music was born in my streets, and you can find beignets and brass bands here.
   Which state am I? _____

3 The first permanent English colony was founded here in 1607 at Jamestown.
   Which state am I? _____

4 You can visit the world's longest cave system — Mammoth Cave — in this state.
Which state am I? _____

5 NASA rockets blast off from my space coast!
   Which state am I? _____

6 Cowboys, wide-open plains, and the Alamo are all part of my story.
   Which state am I? _____

7 My bluegrass music and horse farms make me one of the most beautiful states in the South.
   Which state am I? _____

8 I'm known for my barbecue, blues music, and a mighty river that shares my name.
   Which state am I? _____

9 Visit my Great Smoky Mountains National Park — one of the most-visited parks in the country!
   Which state am I? _____

10 You'll find historic Charleston, sweet tea, and palmetto trees here.
   Which state am I? _____

Matching Game

Famous Places of the South – Match the Place to the State

North Carolina

Cape Hatteras Lighthouse

Texas

Great Smoky Mountains

Tennessee

Mammoth Cave

Kentucky

Charleston Waterfront

Florida

The Alamo

South Carolina

Everglades

Midwest Region

The Midwest is often called the "Heart of America." Known for its farms, friendly towns, and big lakes, this region is the country's center for growing food and transportation. From bustling cities to wide-open plains, the Midwest is full of variety.

Quick Facts

- Largest city: Chicago Illinois
- Number of states: Twelve
- Nickname: "America's Breadbasket"
- Fun Fact: The Midwest has some of the snowiest winters in the United States!

Ohio, Indiana, Illinois, Michigan, Wisconsin, Minnesota, Iowa, Missouri, North Dakota, South Dakota, Nebraska, Kansas

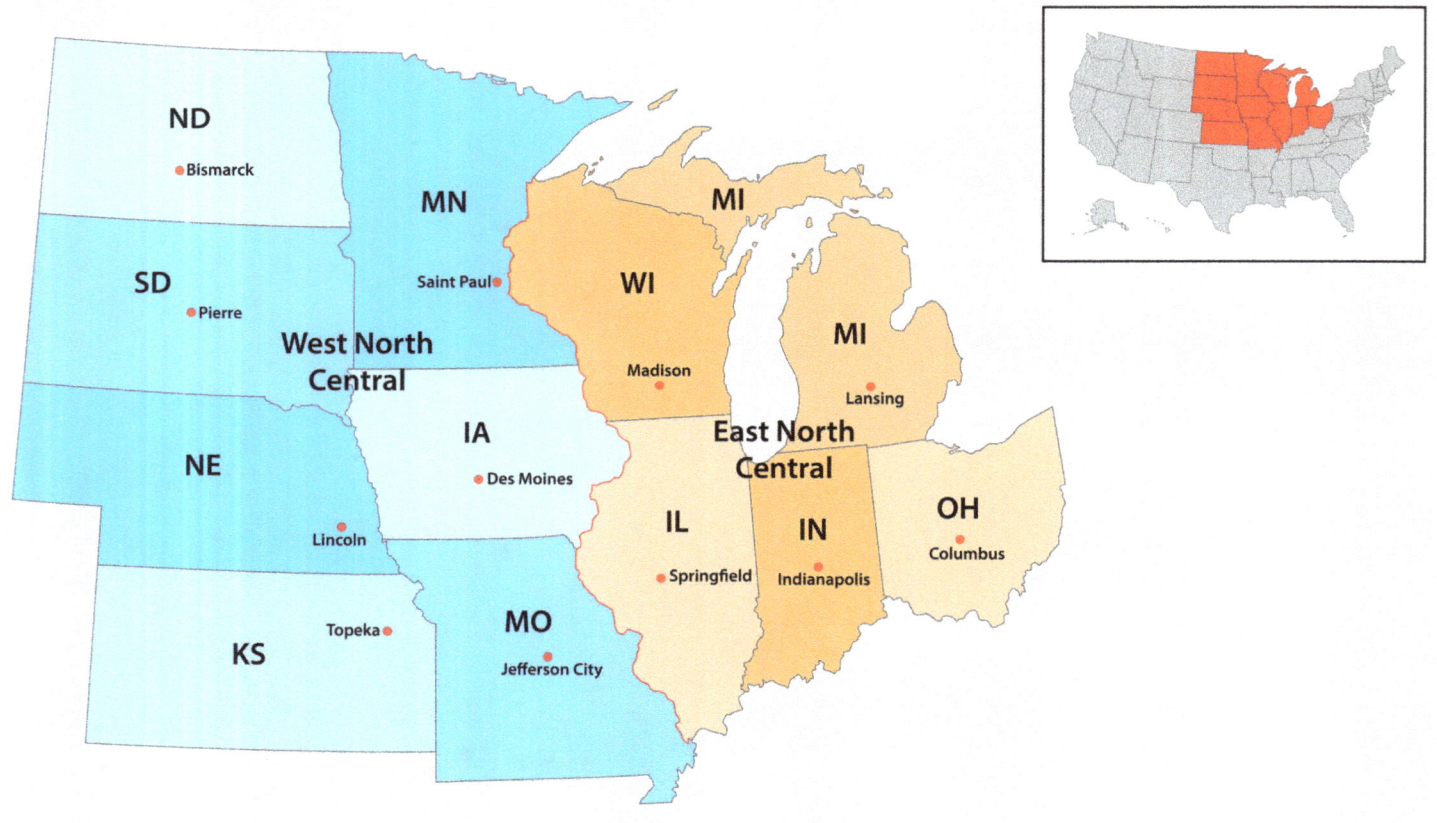

History

The Midwest has long been America's farming center, with Native American cultures, pioneer settlers, and later immigrants all leaving their mark. It's also home to major cities like Chicago and Detroit, which grew during the Industrial Revolution.

Geography

The region is famous for its wide plains, rolling prairies, and the Great Lakes. Summers are hot, winters are cold, and tornadoes sometimes occur in the "Tornado Alley" states.

Culture

The Midwest is known for friendly people, hardworking farming communities, and big cities that celebrate sports, music, and food. It's the birthplace of deep-dish pizza, Motown music, and the ice cream sundae!

Match the Landmark!

Match each Midwestern landmark to its state:

Gateway Arch  _____

Mount Rushmore  _____

Cloud Gate "The Bean"  _____

Rock and Roll Hall of Fame  _____

Illinois

Illinois is known for big cities and wide farmland. Chicago, the state's largest city, sits on Lake Michigan and is famous for skyscrapers, deep-dish pizza, and jazz music. The rest of the state is filled with fields, small towns, and a rich history tied to Abraham Lincoln.

Quick Facts

- ⭐ **Capital:** Springfield
- ✴ **Abbreviation:** IL
- 👤 **Population:** ~12.5 million
- 📅 **Statehood:** 1818 (21st)
- 🏷 **Nickname:** The Prairie State
- 🐦 **Bird:** Northern Cardinal
- 🌸 **Flower:** Violet
- 🐢 **Animal:** White-Tailed Deer
- 📍 **Famous Sites:** Chicago, Abraham Lincoln Home, Route 66

DID YOU KNOW?

The world's first skyscraper was built in Chicago in 1885!

Violet

White-tailed deer

ILLINOIS

State flag

Indiana

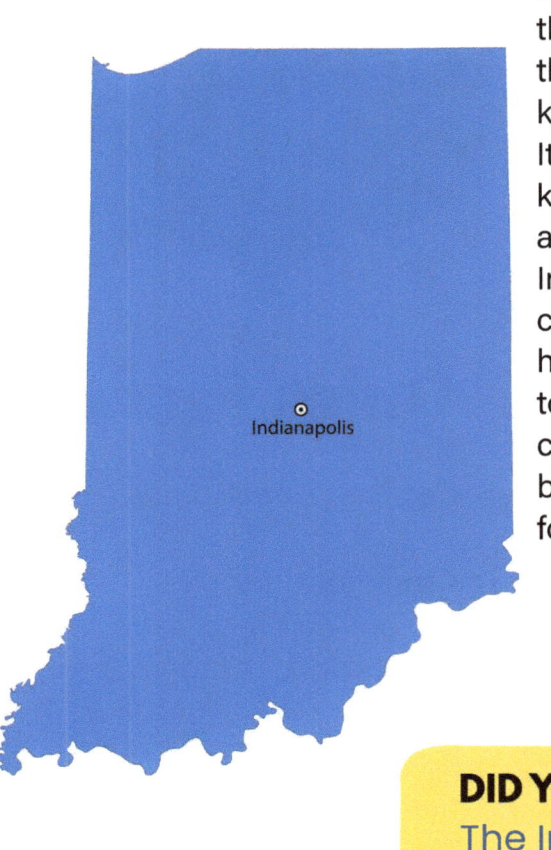

Indiana is called the "Hoosier State," though no one knows exactly why! It's known for basketball, farmland, and the famous Indianapolis 500 car race. The state has a mix of small towns and growing cities surrounded by rolling hills and forests.

Quick Facts

⭐ **Capital:** Indianapolis

🧭 **Abbreviation:** IN

👥 **Population:** ~6.8 million

📅 **Statehood:** 1816 (19th)

🏷️ **Nickname:** The Hoosier State

🐦 **Bird:** Northern Cardinal

🌸 **Flower:** Peony

🐢 **Animal:** Say's firefly

📍 **Famous Sites:** Indianapolis Motor Speedway, Indiana Dunes

DID YOU KNOW?
The Indy 500 car race in Indianapolis is the largest single-day sporting event in the world.

Northern cardinal

Peony

State flag

Iowa

Called the Hawkeye State, Iowa is known for its rolling prairies and golden cornfields. It's one of America's top farming states, but there's more than farmland here—visit Des Moines, explore towns along the Mississippi River, or enjoy the famous Iowa State Fair!

Quick Facts

- ⭐ **Capital:** Des Moines
- 🧭 **Abbreviation:** IA
- 👥 **Population:** ~13.2 million
- 📅 **Statehood:** 1846 (29th)
- 🏷️ **Nickname:** The Hawkeye State
- 🐦 **Bird:** Eastern Goldfinch
- 🌸 **Flower:** Wild Rose
- 🐢 **Animal:** Channel Catfish
- 📍 **Famous Sites:** Field of Dreams, Des Moines Capitol, Amana Colonies

DID YOU KNOW?
Iowa is the only state whose eastern and western borders are both formed by rivers — the Mississippi and the Missouri!

Eastern goldfinch

Wild rose

State flag

Kansas

Kansas is famous for its wide prairies, waving wheat fields, and open skies. It's one of the flattest states, perfect for farming. Known as the "Sunflower State," Kansas is also remembered as the setting of The Wizard of Oz.

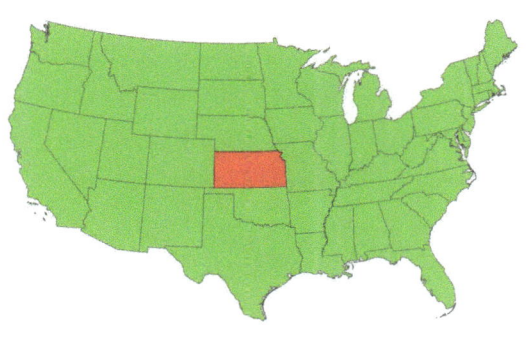

Quick Facts

⭐ **Capital:** Topeka

🧭 **Abbreviation:** KS

👤 **Population:** ~2.9 million

📅 **Statehood:** 1861 (34th)

🏷️ **Nickname:** The Sunflower State

🐦 **Bird:** Western Meadowlark

🌸 **Flower:** Sunflower

🐢 **Animal:** American Bison

📍 **Famous Sites:** Monument Rocks, Dodge City, Wizard of Oz Museum

DID YOU KNOW?
Kansas produces more wheat than almost any other state — enough to bake billions of loaves of bread each year!

Western meadowlark

American bison

State flag

Michigan

Michigan is surrounded by four of the five Great Lakes, giving it more freshwater coastline than any other state. People love to swim, fish, and boat in summer and ski in winter. Detroit, once called the Motor City, helped build America's cars and music.

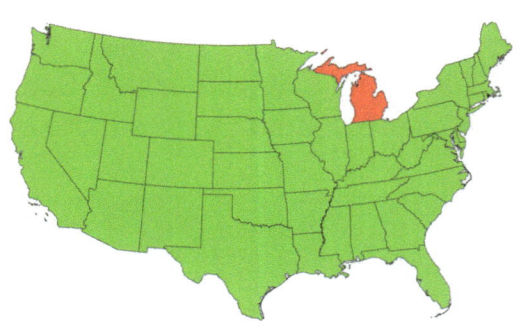

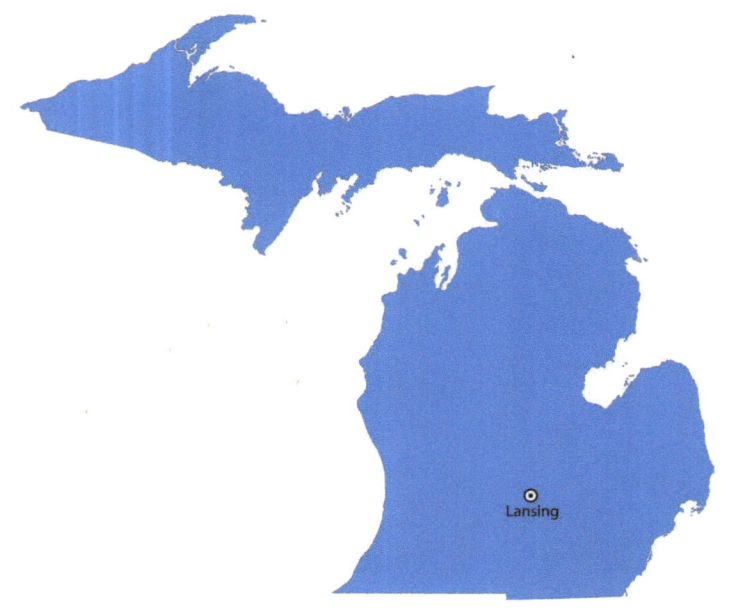

Quick Facts

- ⭐ **Capital:** Lansing
- 🧭 **Abbreviation:** MI
- 👥 **Population:** ~10.1 million
- 📅 **Statehood:** 1837 (26th)
- 🏷️ **Nickname:** The Great Lakes State
- 🐦 **Bird:** American Robin
- 🌸 **Flower:** Apple Blossom
- 🐢 **Animal:** White-Tailed Deer
- 📍 **Famous Sites:** Mackinac Bridge, Detroit, Sleeping Bear Dunes

DID YOU KNOW?
No matter where you stand in Michigan, you're never more than 85 miles from a Great Lake.

American robin

Apple blossom

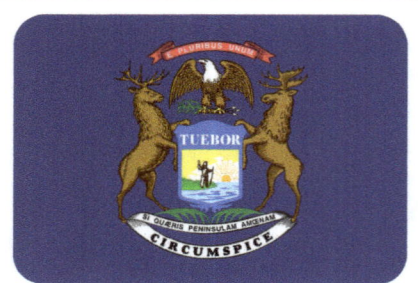

State flag

Minnesota

Minnesota is known as the "Land of 10,000 Lakes" — though it actually has even more! Summers are filled with boating and fishing, while winters bring ice skating and snow sports. The state is also home to the Mall of America, one of the largest malls in the world.

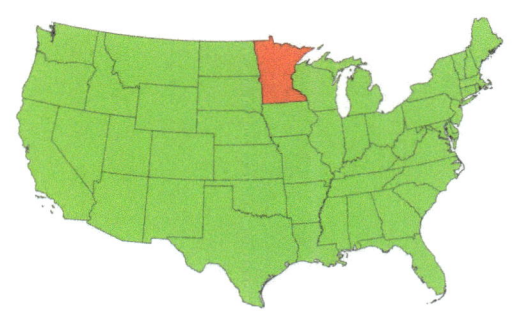

Quick Facts

- ⭐ **Capital:** St. Paul
- 🧭 **Abbreviation:** MN
- 👤 **Population:** ~5.8 million
- 📅 **Statehood:** 1858 (32nd)
- 🏷️ **Nickname:** The Land of 10,000 Lakes
- 🐦 **Bird:** Common Loon
- 🌸 **Flower:** Lady's Slipper
- 🐢 **Animal:** Black Bear
- 📍 **Famous Sites:** Mall of America, Boundary Waters, Split Rock Lighthouse

DID YOU KNOW? The stapler, the pop-up toaster, and the shopping cart were all invented in Minnesota!

Common loon

Black bear

State flag

Missouri

Missouri sits at the crossroads of America, with a mix of plains, forests, and rivers. The Mississippi and Missouri Rivers meet here. The state is known for the Gateway Arch in St. Louis, Kansas City barbecue, and a blend of Southern and Midwestern culture.

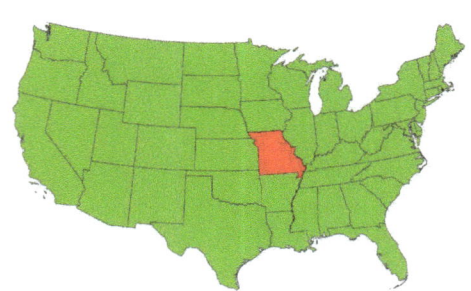

Quick Facts

⭐ **Capital:** Jefferson City

🧭 **Abbreviation:** MO

👤 **Population:** ~6.2 million

📅 **Statehood:** 1821 (24th)

🏷️ **Nickname:** The Show-Me State

🐦 **Bird:** Eastern Bluebird

🌸 **Flower:** Hawthorn

🐢 **Animal:** Missouri Mule

📍 **Famous Sites:** Gateway Arch, Branson, Mark Twain Boyhood Home

DID YOU KNOW?
The Gateway Arch in St. Louis is the tallest man-made monument in the United States.

Eastern bluebird

Hawthorn

State flag

Nebraska

Nebraska's wide-open prairies and rolling sandhills make it one of the most scenic plains states. It's famous for farming, friendly people, and pioneer history. The state's Chimney Rock was a landmark for travelers heading west on the Oregon Trail.

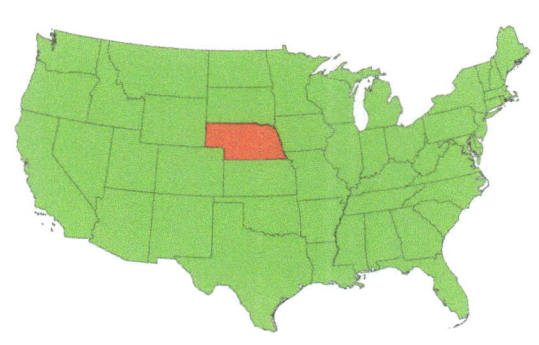

Quick Facts

- ⭐ **Capital:** Lincoln
- 🧭 **Abbreviation:** NE
- 👥 **Population:** ~2 million
- 📅 **Statehood:** 1867 (37th)
- 🏷️ **Nickname:** The Cornhusker State
- 🐦 **Bird:** Western Meadowlark
- 🌸 **Flower:** Goldenrod
- 🦌 **Animal:** White-Tailed Deer
- 📍 **Famous Sites:** Chimney Rock, Carhenge, Scotts Bluff National Monument

DID YOU KNOW?
Kool-Aid was invented in Hastings, Nebraska, in 1927.

Western meadowlark

White-tailed deer

State flag

North Dakota

North Dakota is known for its open plains, beautiful sunsets, and strong farming traditions. It's home to Theodore Roosevelt National Park, where bison and wild horses roam. Winters are cold, but the people are warm and welcoming.

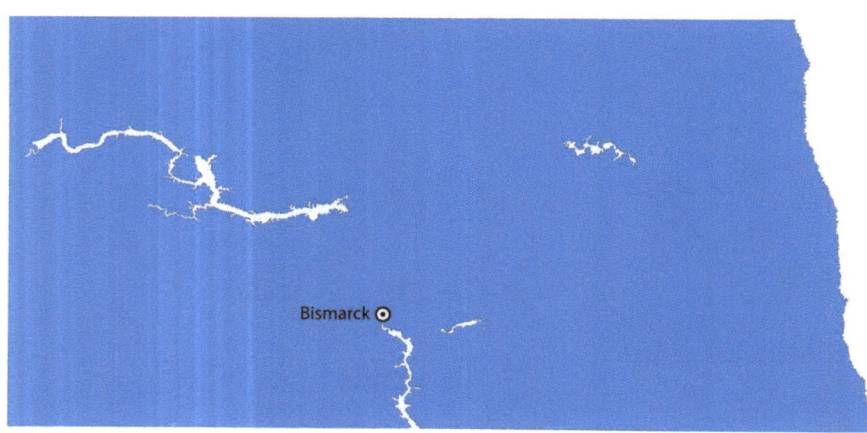

Quick Facts

- ⭐ **Capital:** Bimarck
- 🧭 **Abbreviation:** ND
- 👥 **Population:** ~780,000
- 📅 **Statehood:** 1889 (39th)
- 🏷️ **Nickname:** The Peace Garden State
- 🐦 **Bird:** Western Meadowlark
- 🌸 **Flower:** Wild Prairie Rose
- 🐢 **Animal:** Nokota Horse
- 📍 **Famous Sites:** Theodore Roosevelt National Park, International Peace Garden

DID YOU KNOW?
North Dakota grows more sunflowers than any other state in the country.

Western meadowlark

Wild Prairie Rose

State flag

Ohio

Ohio is full of variety — from big cities like Cleveland and Columbus to peaceful countryside and lakes. It's home to the Rock and Roll Hall of Fame and the birthplace of eight U.S. presidents! Ohio's mix of history, industry, and fun makes it a lively Midwestern state.

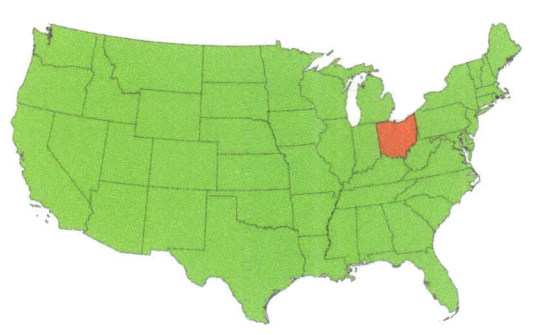

Quick Facts

⭐ **Capital:** Columbus

🧭 **Abbreviation:** OH

👤 **Population:** ~11.8 million

📅 **Statehood:** 1863 (35th)

🏷️ **Nickname:** The Buckeye State

🐦 **Bird:** Northern Cardinal

🌸 **Flower:** Scarlet Carnation

🐢 **Animal:** White-Tailed Deer

📍 **Famous Sites:** Rock & Roll Hall of Fame, Cedar Point, Hocking Hills

DID YOU KNOW?

The first man to walk on the moon, Neil Armstrong, was born in Ohio.

Northern cardinal

White-tailed deer

State flag

South Dakota

South Dakota is famous for Mount Rushmore, where four U.S. presidents are carved into a mountain. The state also has the Badlands, prairies, and buffalo herds. It's a great place for exploring nature and learning about Native American history.

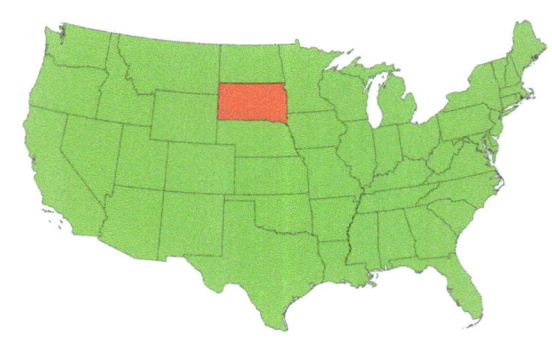

Quick Facts

⭐ **Capital:** Pierre

🧭 **Abbreviation:** SD

👤 **Population:** ~920,000

📅 **Statehood:** 1889 (40th)

🏷️ **Nickname:** The Mount Rushmore State

🐦 **Bird:** Ring-Necked Pheasant

🌸 **Flower:** Pasque Flower

🦎 **Animal:** Coyote

📍 **Famous Sites:** Mount Rushmore, Badlands National Park, Crazy Horse Memorial

DID YOU KNOW?
It took 14 years to carve the faces of four presidents into Mount Rushmore.

Pasque flower

Coyote

State flag

Wisconsin

Wisconsin is known for dairy farms, cheese, and friendly small towns. It borders two Great Lakes, making it perfect for boating and fishing. The state is also known for sports fans, beautiful fall colors, and the fun summer fairs that bring communities together.

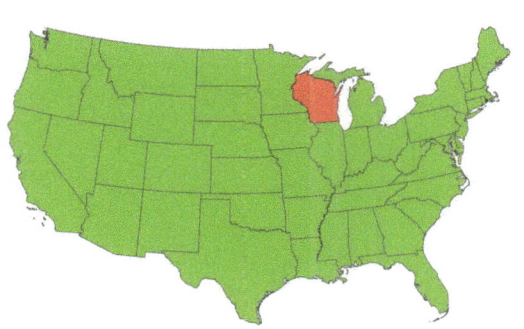

Quick Facts

⭐ **Capital:** Madison

🧭 **Abbreviation:** WI

👥 **Population:** ~5.9 million

📅 **Statehood:** 1848 (30th)

🏷️ **Nickname:** The Badger State

🐦 **Bird:** American Robin

🌸 **Flower:** Wood Violet

🐢 **Animal:** Badger

📍 **Famous Sites:** Milwaukee, Wisconsin Dells, Lambeau Field

DID YOU KNOW?
Wisconsin produces over 600 types of cheese — more than any other state!

American robin

Badger

State flag

67

Word Search

Look for the hidden words in the puzzle below. Can you find them all?

```
G W K I X A T O S E N N I M Y
N Z N R S E R R E I P H Z T N
I D S U K O L D H V D I I N I
S E E O R Z U C O A N C R J S
N A C S A M D T W H N J N K N
A N O S M T A O H O I A V N O
L O L I S O I D S D G O L K C
D R U M I J I R I I A O N Z S
N T M K B K E N H S C K B Z I
E H B W O F L C E N O O V W
B D U A F S I X I S F N H T Z
R A S E M M G L F B J I K Q A
A K J W A K W G H T A B A H Z
S O S I L O P A N A I D N I M
K T S I O N I L L I P G S U L
A A A I H K S A I N T P A U L
U S P R I N G F I E L D S X Q
K O I N D I A N A T O P E K A
```

Bismark	Kansas	North Dakota
Columbus	Lansing	Ohio
Des Moines	Lincoln	Pierre
Illinois	Madison	Saint Paul
Indiana	Michigan	South Dakota
Indianapolis	Minnesota	Springfield
Iowa	Missouri	Topeka
Jefferson City	Nebraska	Wisconsin

Maze Craze

Help the farmer through the barn.

At the Farmer's Market!

The Midwest is known for its friendly towns and fresh, local produce. Explore this busy farmers market and see what you can find! **Bonus: Find the hidden raccoon!**

Which State Am I?

Read each clue and write the name of the state it describes.

1. I'm known as The Prairie State and home to the windy city of Chicago.
   Which state am I? _____

2. You can visit a giant stainless-steel arch in my biggest city — it's called he Gateway Arch!
   Which state am I? _____

3. My name comes from a Native American word for "great river," and my capital is Des Moines.
   Which state am I? _____

4. People say I'm "The Land of 10,000 Lakes," though I actually have even more!
   Which state am I? _____

5. My state borders four of the Great Lakes and is shaped like a mitten.
   Which state am I? _____

6. You can drive across wide prairies and see endless fields of sunflowers here.
   Which state am I? _____

7. One of America's most famous presidents, Abraham Lincoln, grew up here — and we host the Indy 500!
   Which state am I? _____

8. I'm famous for dairy farms and cheese — my football fans even wear foam "cheeseheads"!
   Which state am I? _____

9. You can find Mount Rushmore carved into a granite cliff in this state.
   Which state am I? _____

10. My capital is Bismarck, and I share a peaceful border garden with Canada.
    Which state am I? _____

West Region

The West is the largest region in the United States, stretching from the Great Plains to the Pacific Ocean. It's full of dramatic landscapes — tall mountains, vast deserts, and famous national parks — as well as some of the country's biggest cities.

Montana, Wyoming, Colorado, New Mexico, Arizona, Utah, Idaho, Washington, Oregon, California, Nevada, Alaska, Hawaii

Quick Facts

- Largest city: Los Angeles, California
- Home to the Rocky Mountains, deserts, and the Pacific coastline
- Alaska is larger than Texas, California, and Montana combined.
- Fun Fact: The West has the most national parks of any region!

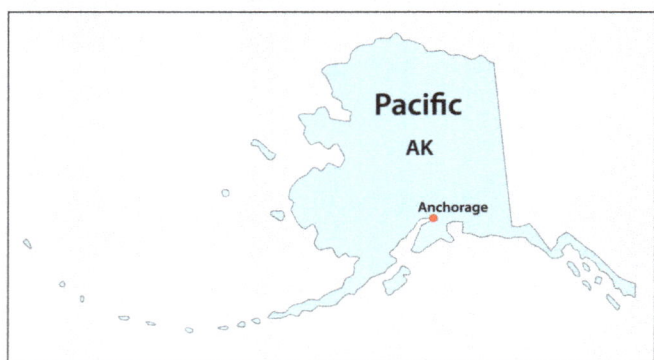
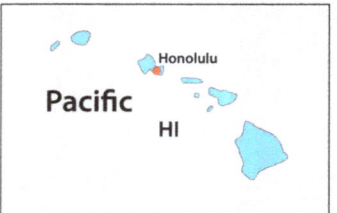
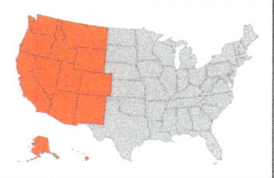

History

The West was once called the "frontier," where pioneers, gold miners, and explorers traveled in search of opportunity. It's also rich in Native American history and culture that shaped the region long before settlers arrived.

Geography

The West has some of America's most famous landscapes: the Rocky Mountains, the Grand Canyon, giant redwood trees, and even active volcanoes. Alaska has glaciers, while Hawaii is made of volcanic islands in the Pacific Ocean.

Culture

The West is a mix of modern and traditional. Cities like Los Angeles, Seattle, and San Francisco are centers of technology and entertainment, while rural areas celebrate cowboy traditions, Native American heritage, and outdoor adventure.

Match the Landmark!

Match each Western landmark to its state:

Grand Canyon   _____

Golden Gate Bridge   _____

Yellowstone National Park   _____

Space Needle   _____

Alaska

Alaska is the largest state in the U.S. and home to glaciers, mountains, and incredible wildlife. People come here to see moose, whales, and the northern lights. Summer days can last nearly all night, while winter brings long, snowy nights and endless adventure.

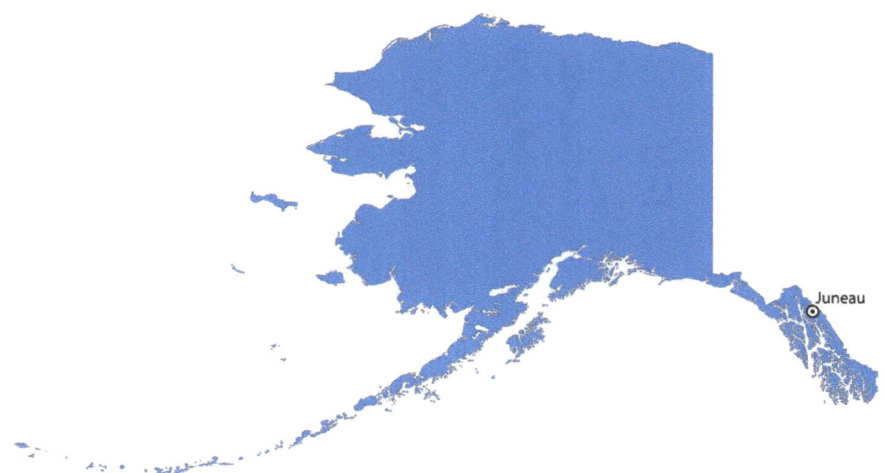

Quick Facts

- ⭐ **Capital:** Juneau
- 🧭 **Abbreviation:** AK
- 👥 **Population:** ~730,000
- 📅 **Statehood:** 1959 (49th)
- 🏷️ **Nickname:** The Last Frontier
- 🐦 **Bird:** Willow Ptarmigan
- 🌸 **Flower:** Forget-Me-Not
- 🐢 **Animal:** Moose
- 🎈 **Famous Sites:** Denali, Glacier Bay, Northern Lights

DID YOU KNOW?

Alaska has more coastline than all the other U.S. states combined — over 33,000 miles!

Willow Ptarmigan

Moose

State flag

Arizona

Arizona is known for its deserts, cacti, and red rock canyons. The Grand Canyon, one of the Seven Natural Wonders of the World, attracts millions of visitors every year. With its warm climate and unique scenery, Arizona is a land of color and contrast.

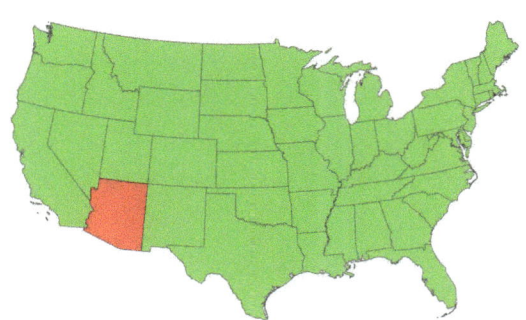

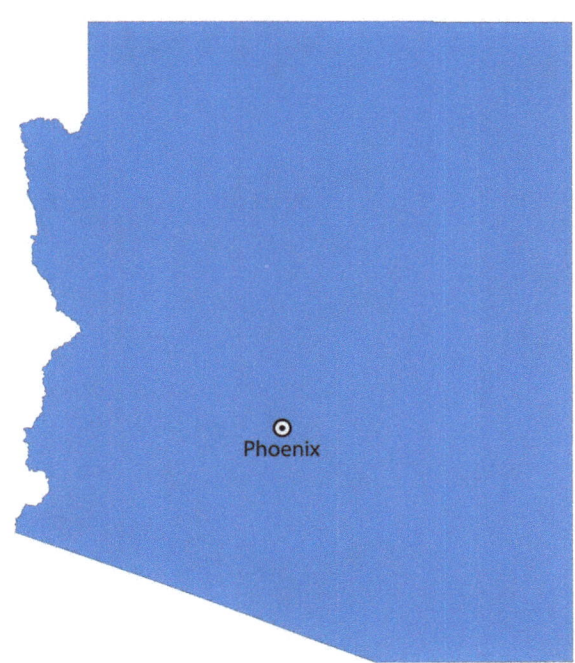

Quick Facts

⭐ **Capital:** Phoenix

🧭 **Abbreviation:** AZ

👥 **Population:** ~7.5 million

📅 **Statehood:** 1912 (48th)

🏷️ **Nickname:** The Grand Canyon State

🐦 **Bird:** Cactus Wren

🌸 **Flower:** Saguaro Cactus Blossom

🐢 **Animal:** Ringtailed Cat

📍 **Famous Sites:** Grand Canyon, Monument Valley, Sedona

DID YOU KNOW?
The Grand Canyon is so deep that you could stack five Empire State Buildings inside it!

Saguaro cactus blossom

Cactus wren

State flag

California

California has it all — beaches, deserts, forests, and mountains. It's home to Hollywood, Silicon Valley, and the giant redwood trees. People come for sunshine, surfing, skiing, and sights like Yosemite National Park and the Golden Gate Bridge. It's one of the most diverse states in the nation.

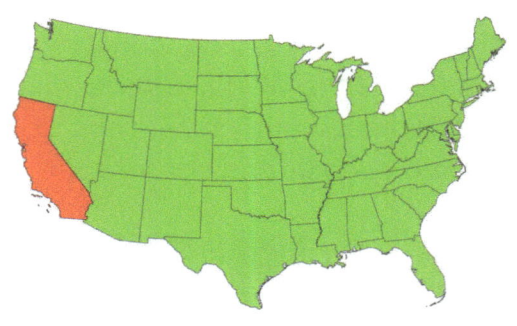

DID YOU KNOW?

California grows more than one-third of all the fruits and vegetables in the United States.

Quick Facts

⭐ **Capital:** Sacramento

🧭 **Abbreviation:** CA

👥 **Population:** ~39 million

📅 **Statehood:** 1850 (31st)

🏷️ **Nickname:** The Golden State

🐦 **Bird:** California Quail

🌸 **Flower:** California Poppy

🐢 **Animal:** Grizzly Bear

📍 **Famous Sites:** Golden Gate Bridge, Yosemite, Hollywood

California poppy

California quail

State flag

Colorado

Colorado is famous for the Rocky Mountains, where people ski, hike, and explore all year long. The Mile High City of Denver sits right at the mountain's edge. The state is also known for clear blue skies, outdoor adventure, and historic gold mining towns.

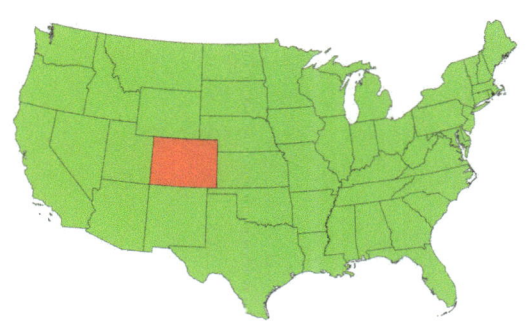

Quick Facts

- ⭐ **Capital:** Denver
- 🧭 **Abbreviation:** CO
- 👤 **Population:** ~5.9 million
- 📅 **Statehood:** 1876 (38th)
- 🏷️ **Nickname:** The Centennial State
- 🐦 **Bird:** Lark Bunting
- 🌸 **Flower:** Rocky Mountain Columbine
- 🐢 **Animal:** Bighorn Sheep
- 📍 **Famous Sites:** Rocky Mountain National Park, Mesa Verde, Pikes Peak

Lark bunting

DID YOU KNOW?
Colorado has over 50 mountain peaks that are higher than 14,000 feet — they're called "fourteeners."

Bighorn sheep

State flag

Hawaii

Hawaii is made up of volcanic islands in the middle of the Pacific Ocean. It's known for beaches, palm trees, and colorful flowers. People visit to surf, hike volcanoes, and experience Hawaiian culture — from hula dancing to luaus filled with island food and music.

Quick Facts

- ⭐ **Capital:** Honolulu
- 🧭 **Abbreviation:** HI
- 👤 **Population:** ~1.4 million
- 📅 **Statehood:** 1959 (50th)
- 🏷️ **Nickname:** The Aloha State
- 🐦 **Bird:** Hawaiian Goose
- 🌸 **Flower:** Yellow Hibiscus
- 🐢 **Animal:** Monk Seal
- 📍 **Famous Sites:** Pearl Harbor, Volcanoes National Park, Waikiki Beach

DID YOU KNOW?
Hawaii is the only U.S. state that grows coffee — and it's picked by hand on volcanic slopes!

Yellow hibiscus

Monk seal

State flag

Idaho

Idaho is famous for its rugged mountains, forests, and, of course, potatoes! The state is full of outdoor adventure, from rafting wild rivers to hiking scenic trails. It's also home to beautiful lakes and friendly small towns that celebrate nature year-round.

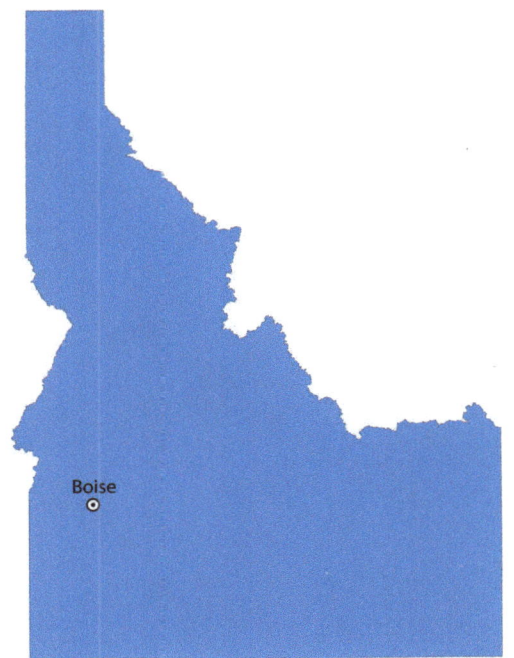

Quick Facts

- ⭐ **Capital:** Boise
- 🧭 **Abbreviation:** ID
- 👥 **Population:** ~2 million
- 📅 **Statehood:** 1890 (43rd)
- 🏷️ **Nickname:** The Gem State
- 🐦 **Bird:** Mountain Bluebird
- 🌸 **Flower:** Syringa
- 🐢 **Animal:** Appaloosa Horse
- 📍 **Famous Sites:** Shoshone Falls, Craters of the Moon, Sun Valley

DID YOU KNOW? Idaho produces about one-third of all the potatoes grown in the United States.

Mountain bluebird

Appaloosa horse

State flag

Montana

Montana is known as "Big Sky Country" for its wide-open spaces and breathtaking views. It's home to Glacier National Park, the Rocky Mountains, and countless ranches. People visit to see wildlife, go fishing, and enjoy the state's quiet beauty and endless skies.

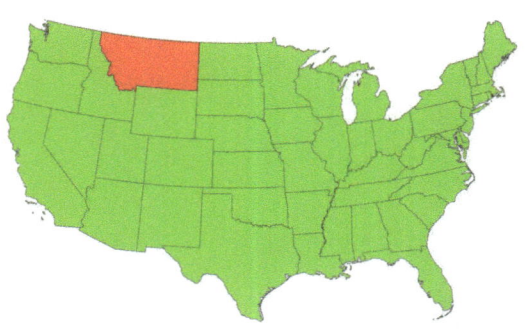

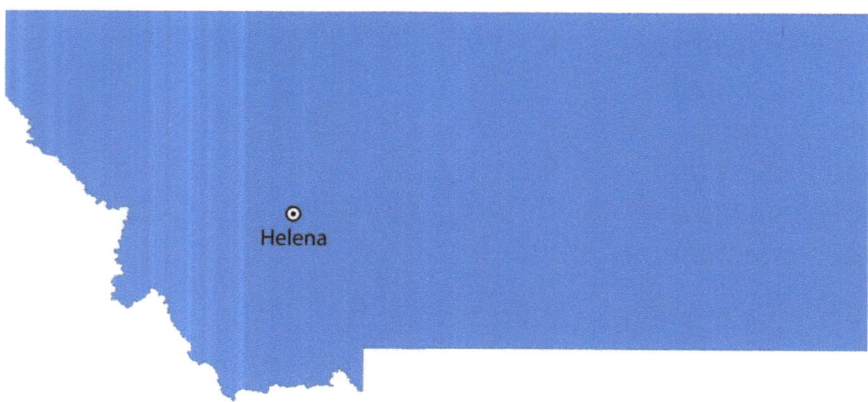

Quick Facts

⭐ **Capital:** Helena

🧭 **Abbreviation:** MT

👥 **Population:** ~1.1 million

📅 **Statehood:** 1889 (41st)

🏷️ **Nickname:** Big Sky Country

🐦 **Bird:** Meadowlark

🌸 **Flower:** Bitterroot

🐢 **Animal:** Grizzly Bear

📍 **Famous Sites:** Glacier National Park, Yellowstone, Little Bighorn Battlefield

DID YOU KNOW?
Montana has more cattle than people — almost three cows for every resident!

Meadowlark

Grizzly bear

State flag

Nevada

Nevada is a state of contrasts — deserts, mountains, and sparkling cities. Las Vegas is famous for its bright lights and entertainment, but the rest of the state offers ghost towns, canyons, and outdoor fun. Lake Tahoe and the Hoover Dam are two of its most popular attractions.

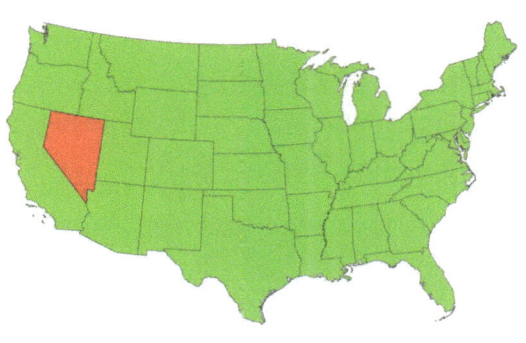

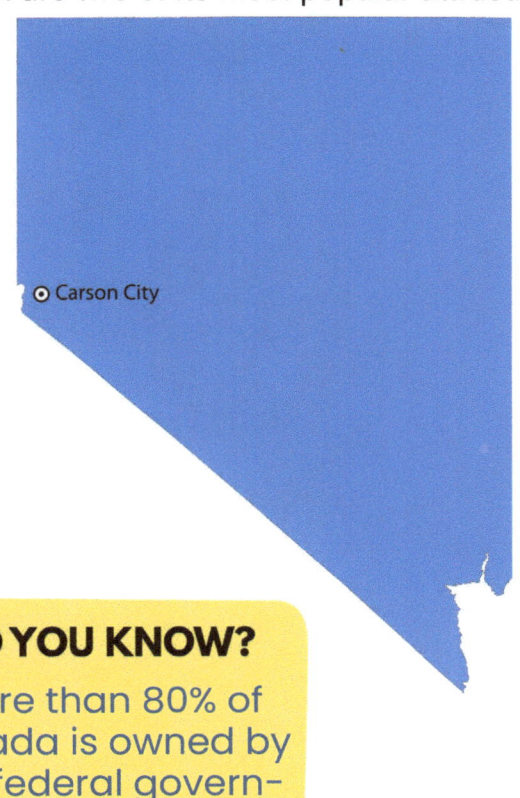

Quick Facts

- ⭐ **Capital:** Carson City
- 🧭 **Abbreviation:** NV
- 👤 **Population:** ~3.2 million
- 📅 **Statehood:** 1864 (36th)
- 🏷️ **Nickname:** The Silver State
- 🐦 **Bird:** Mountain Bluebird
- 🌸 **Flower:** Sagebrush
- 🐢 **Animal:** Bighorn Sheep
- 📍 **Famous Sites:** Las Vegas Strip, Hoover Dam, Lake Tahoe

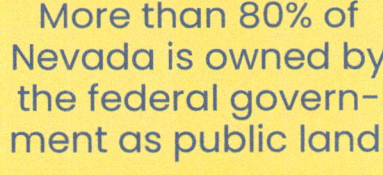

DID YOU KNOW?
More than 80% of Nevada is owned by the federal government as public land.

Bighorn sheep

Mountain bluebird

State flag

New Mexico

New Mexico is called the "Land of Enchantment" for its colorful deserts, mountains, and mix of cultures. It's known for Native American art, ancient pueblos, and spicy food. The state's blend of history, science, and nature makes it truly unique.

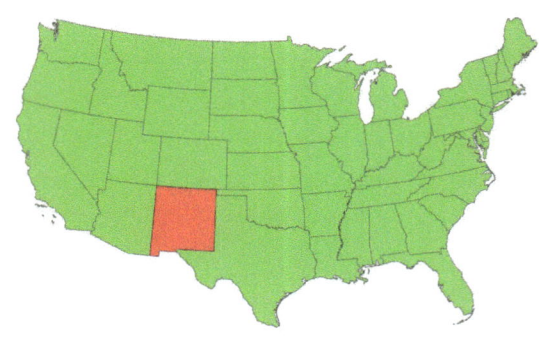

Quick Facts

- ⭐ **Capital:** Santa Fe
- 🧭 **Abbreviation:** NM
- 👥 **Population:** ~2.1 million
- 📅 **Statehood:** 1912 (47th)
- 🏷️ **Nickname:** The Land of Enchantment
- 🐦 **Bird:** Greater Roadrunner
- 🌸 **Flower:** Yucca
- 🐢 **Animal:** Black Bear
- 📍 **Famous Sites:** Carlsbad Caverns, White Sands, Taos Pueblo

Greater roadrunner

DID YOU KNOW?
New Mexico has more PhDs per capita than any other state — thanks to its national labs and research centers!

Black bear

State flag

Oregon

Oregon is full of natural beauty, from the Pacific Ocean to tall forests and volcanic peaks. It's known for waterfalls, coffee, and the city of Portland's creative energy. Outdoor lovers come to hike, camp, and explore its rugged coastline and scenic trails.

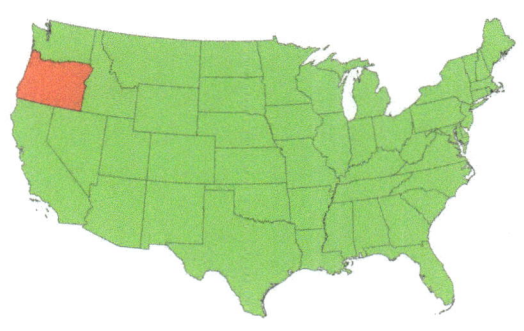

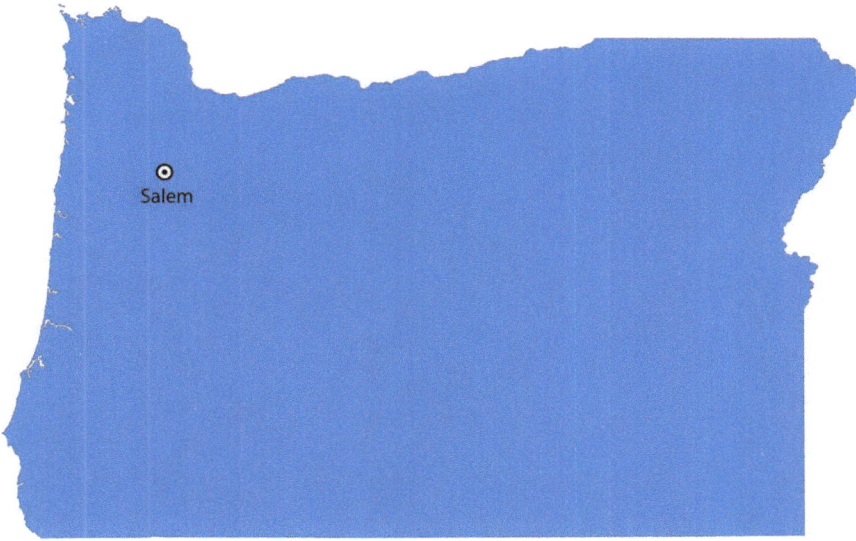

Quick Facts

- ⭐ **Capital:** Salem
- 🧭 **Abbreviation:** OR
- 👥 **Population:** ~4.3 million
- 📅 **Statehood:** 1859 (33rd)
- 🏷️ **Nickname:** The Beaver State
- 🐦 **Bird:** Western Meadowlark
- 🌸 **Flower:** Oregon Grape
- 🐢 **Animal:** Beaver
- 📍 **Famous Sites:** Crater Lake, Columbia River Gorge, Mount Hood

DID YOU KNOW?
Oregon has the deepest lake in the United States — Crater Lake, which formed inside a volcano.

Oregon grape

Beaver

State flag

Utah

Utah is famous for its red rock landscapes and five national parks — called the Mighty 5. Arches, Zion, and Bryce Canyon are among the most stunning places in the U.S. Winter brings snow to the mountains, making Utah a perfect place for skiing, hiking, and exploring.

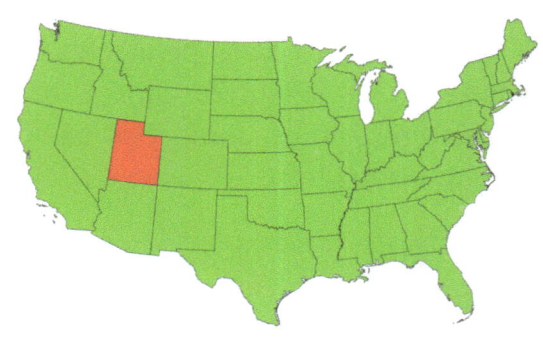

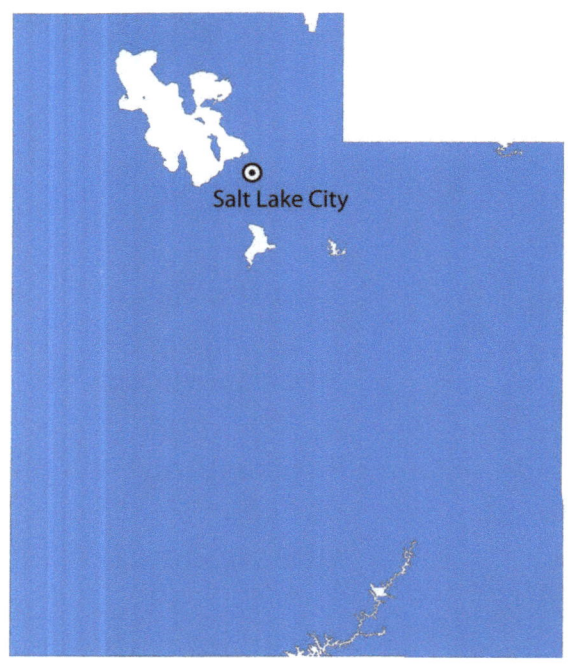

Quick Facts

- ⭐ **Capital:** Salt Lake City
- 🧭 **Abbreviation:** UT
- 👤 **Population:** ~3.5 million
- 📅 **Statehood:** 1896 (45th)
- 🏷️ **Nickname:** The Beehive State
- 🐦 **Bird:** California Gull
- 🌸 **Flower:** Sego Lily
- 🐢 **Animal:** Rocky Mountain Elk
- 📍 **Famous Sites:** Zion, Arches, Bryce Canyon National Parks

California gull

DID YOU KNOW?
Utah's Great Salt Lake is so salty that people can float on the surface without sinking!

Rocky Mountain elk

State flag

Washington

Washington State is a land of forests, mountains, and coastlines. It's home to Seattle, known for coffee, music, and the Space Needle. The state also has volcanoes like Mount Rainier and Mount St. Helens, along with rainy weather that keeps everything green and beautiful.

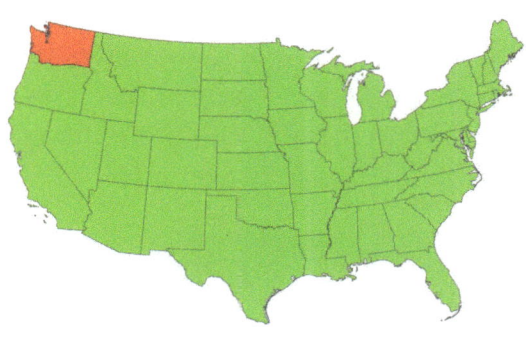

Quick Facts

- ⭐ **Capital:** Olympia
- 🧭 **Abbreviation:** WA
- 👤 **Population:** ~7.8 million
- 📅 **Statehood:** 1889 (42nd)
- 🏷️ **Nickname:** The Evergreen State
- 🐦 **Bird:** Willow Goldfinch
- 🌸 **Flower:** Coast Rhododendron
- 🐢 **Animal:** Orca Whale
- 📍 **Famous Sites:** Space Needle, Mount Rainier, Olympic National Park

DID YOU KNOW?
Washington produces more apples than any other state — over 100 million boxes a year!

Orca whale

Willow goldfinch

State flag

Wyoming

Wyoming is full of natural wonders, including Yellowstone and Grand Teton National Parks. It's known for cowboys, rodeos, and wide-open landscapes. Geysers, mountains, and wildlife make it one of the most beautiful and least crowded states in the country.

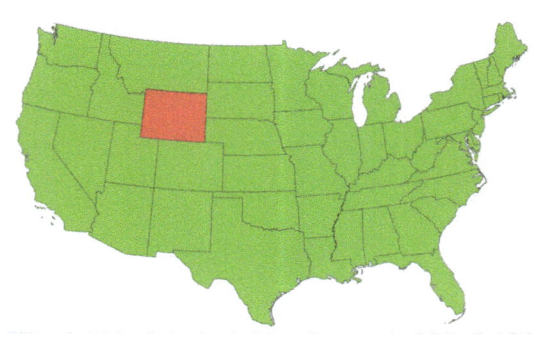

Cheyenne

DID YOU KNOW?
Yellowstone, mostly in Wyoming, became the world's first national park in 1872.

Western meadowlark

American bison

Quick Facts

⭐ **Capital:** Cheyenne

🧭 **Abbreviation:** WY

👥 **Population:** ~580,000

📅 **Statehood:** 1890 (44th)

🏷️ **Nickname:** The Equality State

🐦 **Bird:** Western Meadowlark

🌸 **Flower:** Indian Paintbrush

🐢 **Animal:** American Bison

📍 **Famous Sites:** Yellowstone, Grand Teton, Devil's Tower

State flag

Maze Craze

Find your way from the bottom of the cactus to the top.

Word Search

Look for the hidden words in the puzzle below. Can you find them all?

```
N D X H O N O L U L U T N L Q
E E I Y J Q F U T A H U O X T
V N N F T O R E G O N H N V M
A V E Z R E F A T N A S I F Y
D E O W M R C U N A K S A L A
A R H M S W N H Q H E L E N A
W C P V O O T N E M A R C A S
Y A T G S N F J U Y N R L P H
T L S S A L T L A K E C I T Y
I I C H O K Z A I I N N O E U
C F O Y I T Q I N M E C N A A
N O L T S N A S G A I V E E N
O R O X Z W G N A X X N O B O
S N R H A G I T E L U S H O Z
R I A H S M X M O J E D A I I
A A D P O X W C E N R M D S R
C K O Y S E H W X L E Q I E A
I I W P N F K A I P M Y L O M
```

- Alaska
- Arizona
- Boise
- California
- Carson City
- Cheyenne
- Colorado
- Denver
- Hawaii
- Helena
- Honolulu
- Idaho
- Juneau
- Montana
- Nevada
- New Mexico
- Olympia
- Oregon
- Phoenix
- Sacramento
- Salem
- Salt Lake City
- Santa Fe
- Utah
- Washington
- Wyoming

Which State Am I?

Read each clue and write the name of the state it describes.

1 You can hike through the Grand Canyon and see layers of colorful rock that are millions of years old.
   Which state am I? _____

2 I'm the Golden State — home to surfers, movie stars, and the giant redwood trees.
   Which state am I? _____

3 You'll find geysers, bison, and the first national park in the United States here.
   Which state am I? _____

4 This state is famous for potatoes, mountain lakes, and a city called Boise.
   Which state am I? _____

5 My islands are surrounded by the Pacific Ocean, and you can visit active volcanoes here.
   Which state am I? _____

6 I'm known for my bright lights, desert landscapes, and a city where people shout "Viva!"
   Which state am I? _____

7 Skiers love my snowy mountains, and my capital city's name includes the word "Lake."
   Which state am I? _____

8 My nickname is "Big Sky Country," and you can visit Glacier National Park here.
   Which state am I? _____

9 You can drive through the Rocky Mountains and visit the Mile-High City.
   Which state am I? _____

10 My state bird is the Willow Goldfinch, and you can see Mount Rainier towering above the clouds.
   Which state am I? _____

In the Wild West!

In the 1800s, small towns popped up across the American West. Saloons were gathering places for travelers, ranchers, and prospectors after a long day's work.

FIND 12 HIDDEN OBJECTS IN THE PICTURE

All About America Quiz

1. What is the capital of the United States? _____

2. How many stars are on the U.S. flag?
   A. 13   B. 48   C. 50

3. How many stripes are on the U.S. flag? _____

4. Which ocean borders the East Coast?
   A. Pacific   B. Atlantic   C. Arctic

5. The Liberty Bell is found in which city?
   A. Philadelphia   B. Boston   C. New York

6. Which U.S. state is known as The Sunshine State? _____

7. What is the largest state in the United States? _____

8. Name one of the Great Lakes. _____

9. Which mountain range runs along the western part of the country? _____

10. What are the two countries that border the U.S.? _____

11. What is the national bird of the United States?
    A. Bald Eagle   B. Turkey   C. Hawk

12. What is the nickname of New York City?
    A. The Big Apple   B. The Windy City   C. The Motor City

13. True or False: Mount Rushmore has the faces of four U.S. presidents. _____

14. Which U.S. state is made up of islands? _____

15. What is the official residence of the U.S. president? _____

Capitals Quiz
Write the capital for each state.

Albany	Charleston	Hartford	Madison	Richmond
Atlanta	Cheyenne	Helena	Montgomery	Sacramento
Annapolis	Columbia	Honolulu	Montpelier	St. Paul
Augusta	Columbus	Indianapolis	Nashville	Salem
Austin	Concord	Jackson	Oklahoma City	Salt Lake City
Baton Rouge	Denver	Jefferson City	Olympia	Santa Fe
Bismark	Des Moines	Juneau	Phoenix	Springfield
Boise	Dover	Lansing	Pierre	Tallahassee
Boston	Frankfort	Lincoln	Providence	Topeka
Carlson City	Harrisburg	Little Rock	Raleigh	Trenton

Alabama _____

Alaska _____

Arizona _____

Arkansas _____

California _____

Colorado _____

Connecticut _____

Delaware _____

Florida _____

Georgia _____

Hawaii _____

Idaho _____

Illinois _____

Indiana _____

Iowa _____

Kansas _____

Kentucky _____

Louisiana _____

Maine _____

Maryland _____

Massachusetts _____

Michigan _____

Minnesota _____

Mississippi _____

Missouri _____

Montana _____

Nebraska _____

Nevada _____

New Hampshire _____

New Jersey _____

New Mexico _____

New York _____

North Carolina _____

North Dakota _____

Ohio _____

Oklahoma _____

Oregon _____

Pennsylvania _____

Rhode Island _____

South Carolina _____

South Dakota _____

Tennessee _____

Texas _____

Utah _____

Vermont _____

Virginia _____

Washington _____

West Virginia _____

Wisconsin _____

Wyoming _____

USA Maze
Find your way across the USA!

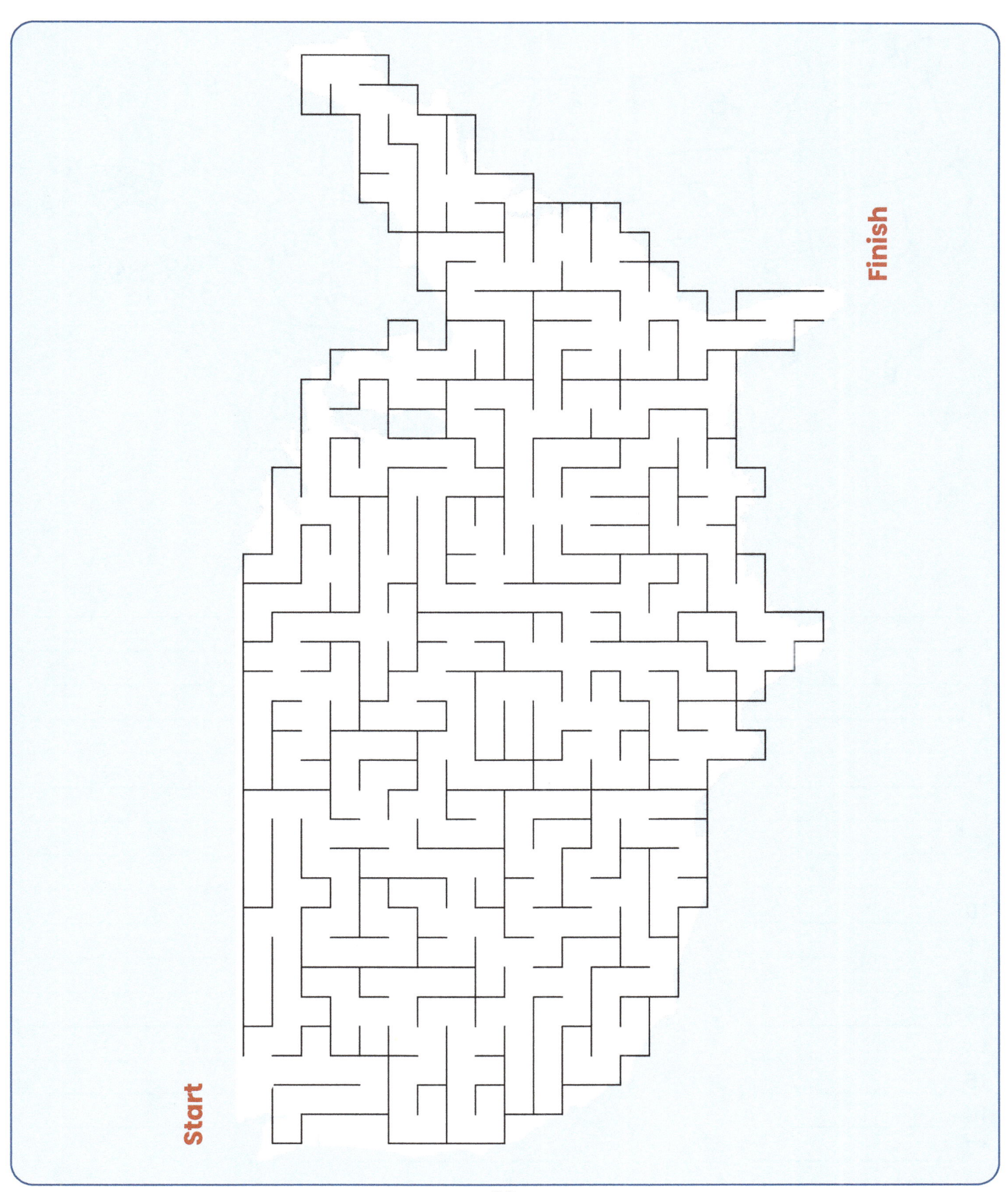

Map Quiz

Do you remember where each state is on the map?

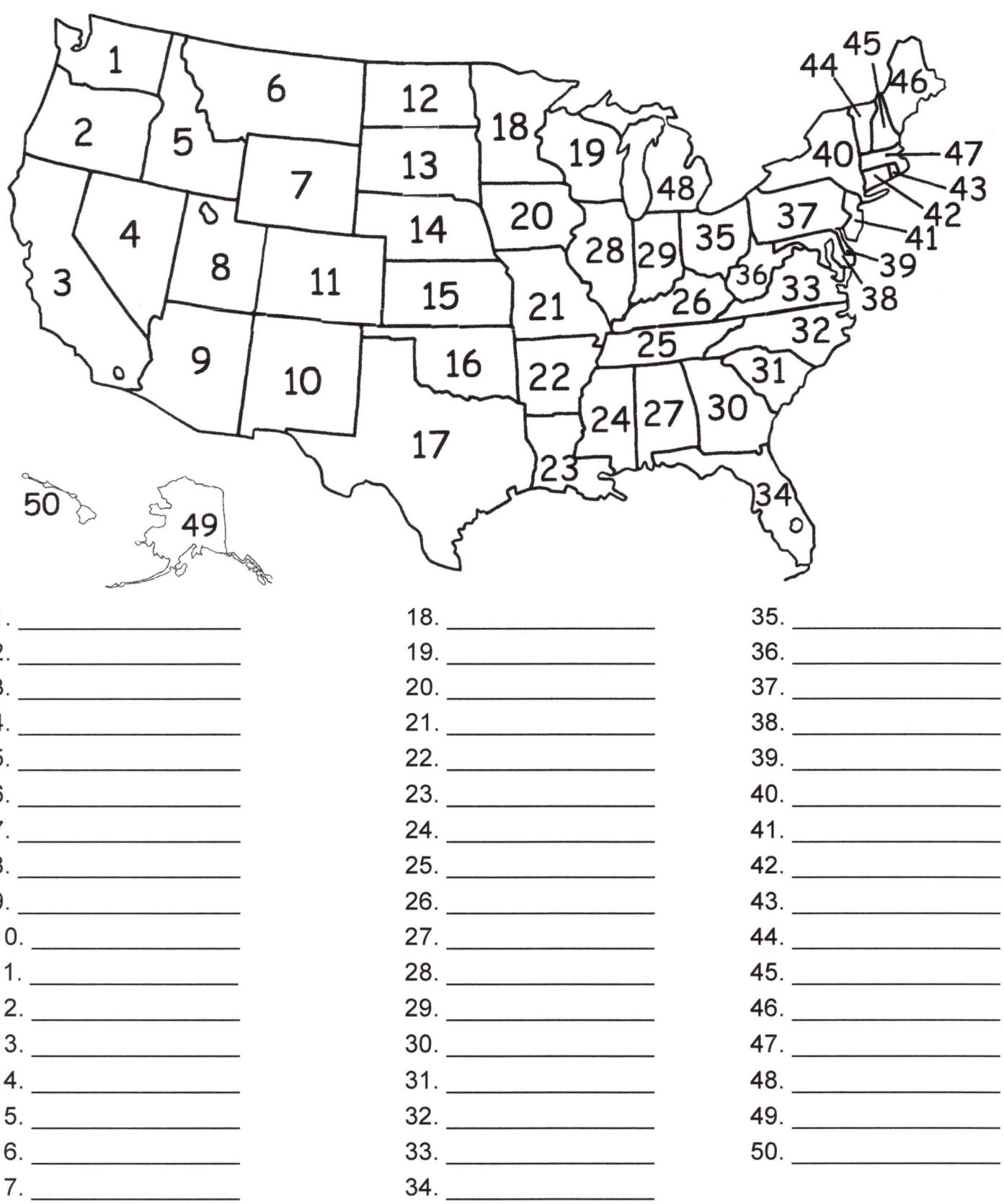

1. _____
2. _____
3. _____
4. _____
5. _____
6. _____
7. _____
8. _____
9. _____
10. _____
11. _____
12. _____
13. _____
14. _____
15. _____
16. _____
17. _____
18. _____
19. _____
20. _____
21. _____
22. _____
23. _____
24. _____
25. _____
26. _____
27. _____
28. _____
29. _____
30. _____
31. _____
32. _____
33. _____
34. _____
35. _____
36. _____
37. _____
38. _____
39. _____
40. _____
41. _____
42. _____
43. _____
44. _____
45. _____
46. _____
47. _____
48. _____
49. _____
50. _____

U.S. State Capitals Quick Reference

State	Capital	State	Capital
Alabama	Montgomery	Montana	Helena
Alaska	Juneau	Nebraska	Lincoln
Arizona	Phoenix	Nevada	Carson City
Arkansas	Little Rock	New Hampshire	Concord
California	Sacramento	New Jersey	Trenton
Colorado	Denver	New Mexico	Santa Fe
Connecticut	Hartford	New York	Albany
Delaware	Dover	North Carolina	Raleigh
Florida	Tallahassee	North Dakota	Bismarck
Georgia	Atlanta	Ohio	Columbus
Hawaii	Honolulu	Oklahoma	Oklahoma City
Idaho	Boise	Oregon	Salem
Illinois	Springfield	Pennsylvania	Harrisburg
Indiana	Indianapolis	Rhode Island	Providence
Iowa	Des Moines	South Carolina	Columbia
Kansas	Topeka	South Dakota	Pierre
Kentucky	Frankfort	Tennessee	Nashville
Louisiana	Baton Rouge	Texas	Austin
Maine	Augusta	Utah	Salt Lake City
Maryland	Annapolis	Vermont	Montpelier
Massachusetts	Boston	Virginia	Richmond
Michigan	Lansing	Washington	Olympia
Minnesota	St. Paul	West Virginia	Charleston
Mississippi	Jackson	Wisconsin	Madison
Missouri	Jefferson City	Wyoming	Cheyenne

Answers

p. 7

p. 11
Mini-Quiz
b, b, a, b, False

p. 11
Who Am I
b, b, b, a, b

p. 11

p. 13

p. 15
Match the President
1-C, 2-D, 3-B, 4-E, 5-A

Who Was It
1. George Washington
2. Abraham Lincoln
3. Theodore Roosevelt
4. John F. Kennedy
5. Donald Trump

p. 16

p. 19
Match the Landmark
New York
Pennsylvania
Massachusetts
Vermont

p. 29

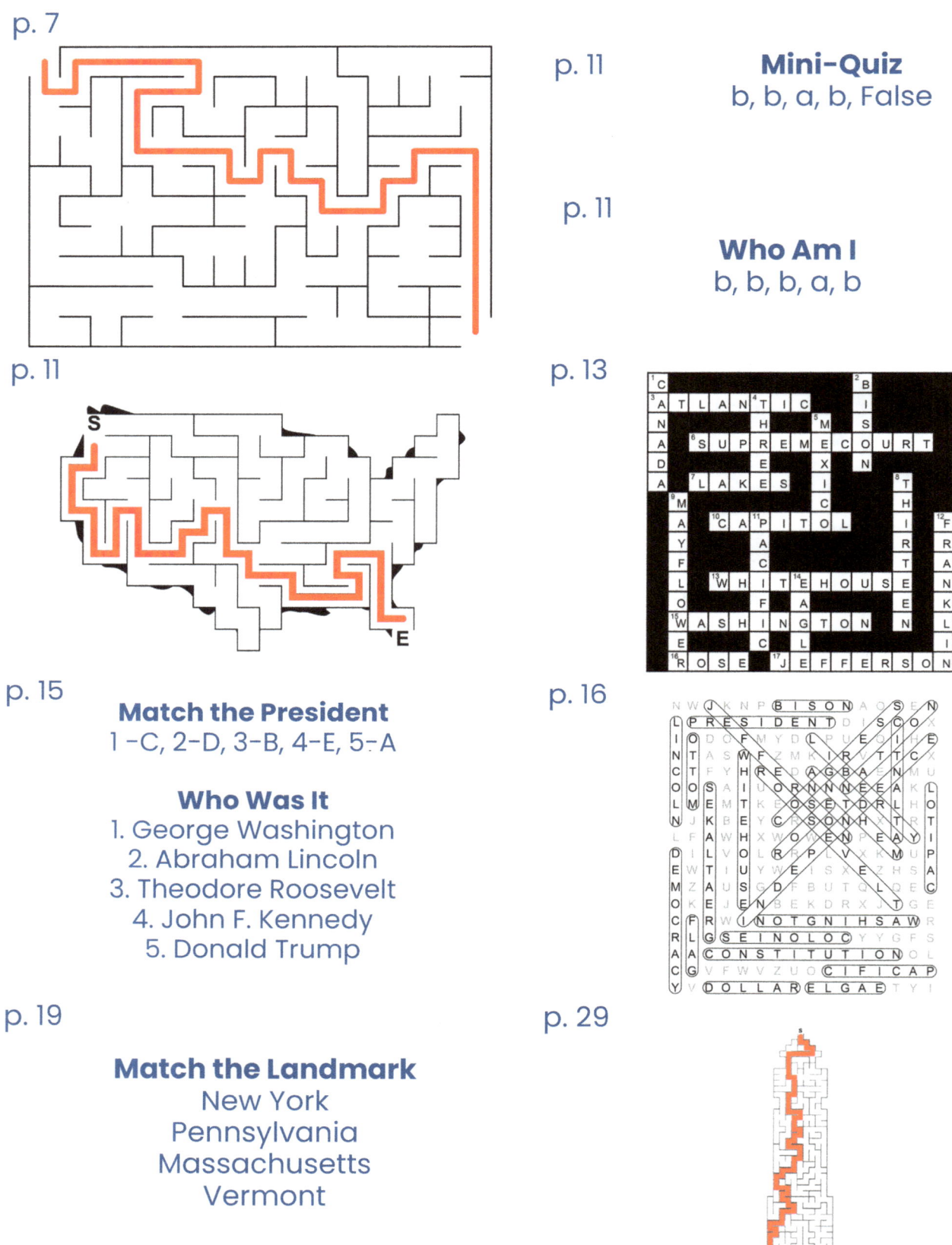

p. 30

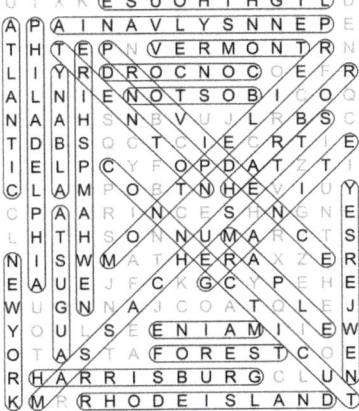

p. 31

Matching Game

Maine - Moose, Rhode Island - Harbor Seal, Vermont - Morgan Horse, New Hampshire - Purple Finch, New York - Beaver, Pennsylvania - Ruffled Grouse, Massachusetts - Right Whale, Connecticut - American Robin, New Jersey - Eastern Goldfinch

p. 33

Match the Landmark

Texas
Florida
Washington, D.C.
Louisiana

p. 50

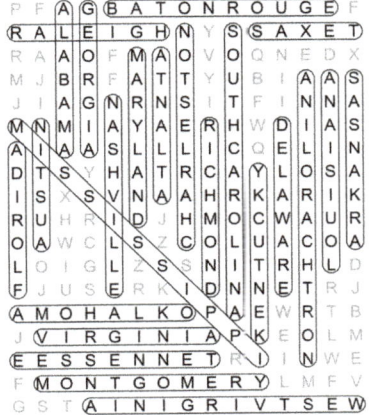

p. 51

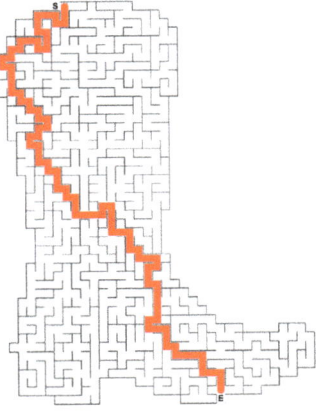

p. 52

Which State Am I?

1. Georgia
2. Louisiana
3. Virgi bostonia
4. Kentucky
5. Florida
6. Texas
7. Kentucky
8. Mississippi
9. Tennessee
10. South Carolina

p. 53

Matching Game

North Carolina - Cape Hatteras
Texas - The Alamo
Tennessee - Great Smoky Mts
Kentucky - Mammoth Caves
Florida - Everglades
South Carolina - Charleston

p. 55

Match the Landmark

Missouri
South Dakota
Illinois
Ohio

p. 68

p. 69

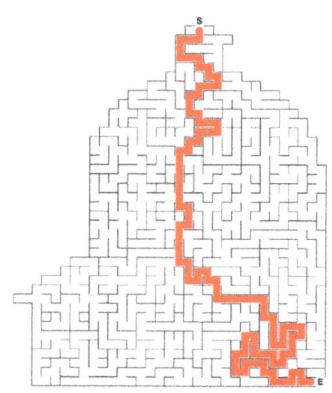

Which State Am I?
1. Illinois
2. Missouri
3. Iowa
4. Minnesota
5. Michigan
6. Kansas
7. Indiana
8. Wisconsin
9. South Dakota
10. North Dakota

p. 70

p. 71

p. 73

Match the Landmark

Arizona
California
Wyoming
Washington

p. 87

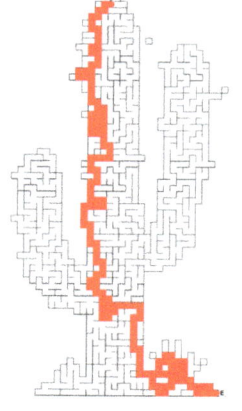

p. 88

p. 89

Which State Am I?
1. Arizona
2. California
3. Wyoming
4. Idaho
5. Hawaii
6. Nevada
7. Utah
8. Montana
9. Colorado
10. Washington

98

p. 90

p. 91

America Quiz
1. Washington, D.C.
2. 50
3. 13
4. Atlantic Ocean
5. Philadelphia
6. Florida
7. Alaska
8. Any of: Superior, Michigan, Huron, Erie, Ontario
9. Rocky Mountains
10. Canada and Mexico
11. Bald Eagle
12. The Big Apple
13. True
14. Hawaii
15. The White House

p. 92

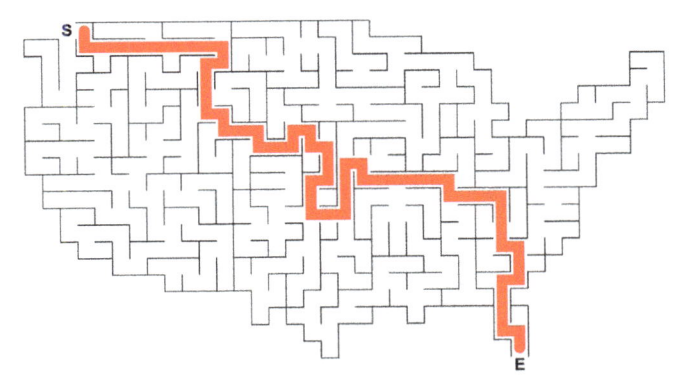

Alabama - Montgomery
Alaska - Juneau
Arizona - Phoenix
Arkansas - Little Rock
California - Sacramento
Colorado - Denver
Connecticut - Hartford
Delaware - Dover
Florida - Tallahassee
Georgia - Atlanta
Hawaii - Honolulu
Idaho - Boise
Illinois - Springfield
Indiana - Indianapolis
Iowa - Des Moines
Kansas - Topeka
Kentucky - Frankfort
Louisiana - Baton Rouge
Maine - Augusta
Maryland - Annapolis
Massachusetts - Boston
Michigan - Lansing
Minnesota - Saint Paul
Mississippi - Jackson
Missouri - Jefferson City
Montana - Helena
Nebraska - Lincoln
Nevada - Carson City
New Hampshire - Concord
New Jersey - Trenton
New Mexico - Santa Fe
New York - Albany
North Carolina - Raleigh
North Dakota - Bismarck
Ohio - Columbus
Oklahoma - Oklahoma City
Oregon - Salem
Pennsylvania - Harrisburg
Rhode Island - Providence
South Carolina - Columbia
South Dakota - Pierre
Tennessee - Nashville
Texas - Austin
Utah - Salt Lake City
Vermont - Montpelier
Virginia - Richmond
Washington - Olympia
West Virginia - Charleston
Wisconsin - Madison
Wyoming - Cheyenne

p. 93

p. 94

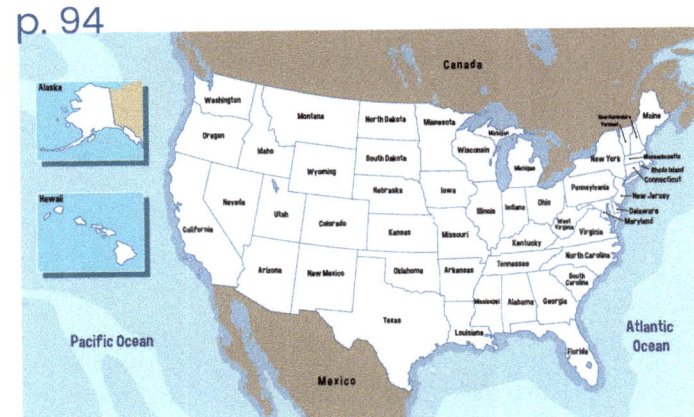

www.ingramcontent.com/pod-product-compliance
Lightning Source LLC
Chambersburg PA
CBHW051257110526
44589CB00025B/2864